LESS EGO, MORE SOUL

A Modern Reinvention Guide
for Women

Janet Ioli

*Search Your Soul and Make Changes
in 21 Days*

Copyright © 2020 by Janet Ioli

Printed in the United States of America
First Printing, 2020
ISBN 978-0-578-70205-6
JI International

"Tear off the mask. Your face is glorious..."
—Rumi

LESS EGO, MORE SOUL

A Modern Reinvention Guide for Women

Table of Contents

When you feel stuck or fixed in your ways, reinvention seems unimaginable, even unattainable. But what if you could define your life to be more fluid, curious, and exuberant? What if you were gently led through activities of introspection and empowerment in the setting of your choice, without an audience or need for any preparation? Deep, impactful change toward the breath of new life. Ultimate alignment of heart, mind, soul. It sounds breathtaking, doesn't it?

Your guided journey in this book will prompt you to let go of incessant pleasing, proving, and polishing. You will integrate the voice of your inner wise woman into a declaration of who you are, what you believe, and what you are committed to. The personal manifesto you will create here is a decision-making and alignment tool for the actions of not the person you are now—but of the person you are becoming.

Live and lead with less ego and more soul.

PART I. THE MASQUERADE

Less Ego, More Soul

Chapter 1

A Day in Your Life

Your alarm buzzes you out of your restless slumber. It's 5:30 a.m. You hit the snooze button and groan.

Is it time to get up already? It seems like you just got to sleep. The digital numbers 12:30 still remain imprinted in your mind's eye as the memory of when your head hit your pillow just a few hours ago.

The alarm goes off again. Has it been ten minutes already? You hear a moan next to you as your partner rolls out of the bed and stumbles towards the bathroom.

Coffee. You really need a caffeine jolt to jump start you out of your numb stupor.

And so, another day begins.

You have a list of things to pick up, errands to run, and too many places to chauffeur your kids to. Your partner and you divide and conquer—your partner owns part of the to-do list you scribbled out last night, with detailed instructions on what to do each step of the way. You breathe out a sigh of relief when you realize that it is his turn to drop the kids off and pick them up today.

Less Ego, More Soul

After a frenzied breakfast drama involving what everyone is wearing to school, you reach into your purse and offer up money to your kids to buy their lunches today. You realize you forgot to pick up bread for lunch sandwiches, but are relieved because you need an early start to work anyway. They are thrilled because it is pizza day in the cafeteria, so no one complains. *Pizza isn't the healthiest food option*, you think to yourself, and then proceed to listen to your internal mind rant about what a terrible mother you are and how other mothers make their kids healthy, Instagram-worthy lunches to take to school every day. You vow to do better—but that's for another time. You quickly peck everyone on the cheek, including your husband as you grab your handbag and rush to your car.

You pause to look in the mirror near the front door—and let out another deep sigh when you see your hair. Why does my hair frizz up like this, you think, and images of women with straight, gorgeous locks on television play in your head. I need to get a new hairstyle this weekend.

The traffic is horrendous and you are fifteen minutes late for your first meeting at work. You try to collect your thoughts and maintain your focus through the back-

4

to-back meeting line-up crammed into your already overflowing calendar.

Time for lunch comes and goes. When you start to feel light-headed around 2:30 pm, you make a mad dash to the office vending machine and treat yourself to whatever processed delight curbs the drug addict-like carbohydrate cravings from your blood sugar crash.

It's 4:30 already and you are now waiting at the dentist's office—proud that you slipped away from the office and have made it on time to your teeth cleaning appointment today even if it is a year overdue. You notice an ad for Aruba as you flip through the magazine sitting on the table in the waiting room and begin to daydream about going on vacation and sitting on the beach in Aruba.

Ah…. The sight of the ocean in your mind's eye begins to relax your body. Suddenly, a wave of anxiety interrupts your vision and spreads over you. Your thoughts have shifted to an internal image of yourself in your blue bathing suit and are showing you the bulges the extra ten pounds you've gained over the winter have added to your physique.

A feeling of disgust and anxiety rushes over you.

I need to find time to exercise, you remind yourself and sigh again. You think of the fittest moms you know and tell yourself how inadequate you are in the fitness and appearance arena. I have let myself go, you deduce as the image of a former version of yourself appears in your head.

Exercise. Yet another thing to add to your list of way too many things to do. Another even stronger wave of anxiety swells in your chest. You can feel the stress mounting to a crescendo. Your shoulders tighten up and begin to send pain up your neck. I need a massage, you think. But who has time for a massage?

You spend an hour in bumper to bumper traffic getting home in the middle of rush hour just in time to warm up Sunday night leftovers for tonight's dinner, try to help your kids with their seemingly foreign homework, get them to bed, and discuss the rest of the week's logistics with your partner. After you and your partner doze sporadically while you watch the latest episode of "The Voice", you summon the energy to get off the couch, throw a load of laundry in the washer, and head to bed.

This is a typical day in your life.

But hey, this is not a bad picture. You are doing a pretty good job at managing your life and keeping things together. You are planning, controlling, administering, and completing most of the tasks you have set out for yourself, aren't you? You have a decent paying job, have made your way up the ranks to a mid-level management position leading a team of people, and you have a nice house, a good spouse, and your kids don't want for much. You have established workable routines and are getting everything you need and should get done, done. You should be grateful and happy. You should be satisfied.

Less Ego, More Soul

Chapter 2

The Voice

If you're like most of the women I've talked to in my work helping leaders lead and grow over the past twenty years, others would describe you as capable, confident, and successful. You make things happen and work hard to have it all and be it all to everyone. By all conventional standards, you're solid and are doing all the things you have learned to define success by.

You are accustomed to rationalizing your behaviors and following what others do. You make compromises and make do, get by, and tell yourself to be happy with what you are doing. You shouldn't expect much more. You compare yourself to others and believe you measure up. You are doing what everyone expected you to do and then some. You probably don't spend much time reflecting on who you are and if you are being true to your wisest self. You are accustomed to being on the surface more than going too deep. All our lives, we watch those around us settling for the surface.

We become accustomed to role models who don't quite live up to the role they are modeling.

Less Ego, More Soul

We become accustomed to leaders who don't live up to our expectations. We then join the world of work and have a vision in our minds of what our leaders will be like. We look around and see that many of the senior executives don't act the way we imagined. They just don't always model the behaviors that inspire us to connect and follow. As a matter of fact, neither do our politicians or even leaders of other major institutions. There is a disconnect between what is stated as valued and what is actually practiced. Keeping up appearances and more surface measures become the standards we look towards—yet something seems to be out of a deeper alignment. Something is off between what our inner wisdom is trying to tell us is important and what we see and do in practice.

Subsequently, we become accustomed to expecting less of ourselves and not holding ourselves accountable to living and leading a life aligned with that voice deep inside of us that knows what is most important and guides us to more. We become accustomed to the "shoulds" that we are socialized with, and create a life around appearing to fulfill those. We learn to please others, prove our worthiness, and polish our outer appearance. We build an identity mask to present to the world that ensures our safety and survival and helps us feel safe, included, and important. After all, we want to be successful, worthy, included, and accepted.

If we really drilled down and looked at our own lives, we might see a glaring misalignment. We often live our lives reactively, run around crazily, and don't make the time for what we say is important. We are often grumpy and tired and react from a place of stress. We don't make enough time to savor the fleeting and simple moments or fully participate in and enjoy them. We don't behave according to the values we say we hold dear and espouse. We say that family, friends, and our health are most important to us, yet we neglect our health and annual physicals, eat unhealthy food, and leave regular connection with our families and friends to chance or to "when we have the time". We say we care about others and are compassionate, yet our actual behaviors are exclusive and judgmental. Years pass and we are still living according to many of the "shoulds" we have created in our lives and established as our doctrine. We still don the façade of appearance and judge our success and the success of others based on the conventional norms we have been socialized with from others who are participating in this same masquerade ball.

Less Ego, More Soul

We all participate in one grand and glorious masquerade —parading, cavorting, and dancing with each other, behind our carefully crafted masks, in a brilliantly choreographed ball.

The years pass and the behaviors we exhibit don't necessarily embody the person we want to be or the life we want to live. We are too tired or too overwhelmed to even think about doing one more thing, much less doing some serious introspection about who we want to be, what is out of alignment, and what we really want to get from our lives. We are too tired and too comfortable to change. We think we are doing the best we can, and that what we are doing is pretty darn good by conventional standards. We get so caught up in all the doing. Day-to-day routines and dramas consume us. We lose sight of how much bigger we are.

And yet when we are alone and have time to think deeply about who we are becoming, there is a knowing voice that calls to us. It is often a whisper, yet it feels like a plea from somewhere deep within us.

"Pay attention," it whispers.

"Listen," it pleads.

The voice causes us discomfort, as it causes us to pause and think more deeply. "Who are you?" it cajoles.

"Are you living in alignment with what is most important?"

"I'm calling you to change your ways. Something is off."

You are off kilter when you hear this voice. It shakes you to the core and even annoys you because it disturbs your sense of comfort and control. You must silence it.

You are doing fine. You are happy just the way things are. You are grateful for what you have, what you have accomplished, and who you have become. You push a chair against the inner portal it comes from and keep yourself busy and distracted. You have it all under control.

This place that calls out to you is a place within you of great power. You know the place. It is your inner wisdom. Some people call it a soul. It doesn't matter what you call it. You know you have felt its presence throughout your life. It has been trying to command your attention with whispers for as long as you can remember. Sometimes you made time to sit and listen. Often, it was steering you somewhere or querying something. More often than not, it was redirecting you or questioning your choices. The challenge scared you. You blocked it out.

What inhibits you from getting to know and fully listen to your inner wise self over the years? It is important for you to understand this piece, for that knowledge can help you shift to reinvention.

> "This place that calls out to you is a place within you of great power.
> You know the place.
> It is your inner wisdom.
> Some people call it a soul."

Chapter 3

The Mask

As of this writing, in the exploration of what inhibits your ability to tap into and listen to the deeper inner wisdom that lies within you, the universe plays out a dramatic irony to emphasize my point. The U.S. Centers for Disease Control has recently advised the general public to wear protective cloth masks on our faces when we go outside our homes. Not only in the United States, but all around the world. We are in the midst of a global pandemic threatening our physical health and livelihoods. We are fearful of being around others as to not catch an invisible COVID-19 virus that is highly contagious. It has not only the potential to make us gravely ill, but to even cause death as it has for many around the globe. People all over the world are wearing some sort of protective mask over their mouths and noses to protect their own and the collective physical health of others.

The irony of this need to now wear a mask is eerily coincidental. You see, what I was going to talk about as the main obstacle that prevents you from accessing your inner wise self is the mask you have created and wear as yourself. You are already wearing a psychological mask of your own making every single day. It is not made of cloth, you can't see it, and you don't put it over your face.

You spend years making it, perfecting it, and polishing it to be just right. You mold it and interchange its features for different times as needed, but certainly don't go anywhere or do or say anything without it. This mask helps you feel safe, worthy, smart, successful, and accepted. This uniquely and carefully crafted masterpiece of your own creation is as vital to your psychological survival as oxygen, and you dare not take it off. It becomes so much a part of yourself that you don't know who you are without it. You reject any part of yourself that doesn't fit with the image of this mask you are wearing.

You and this identity mask you create—are one. You interact with others from behind the protection of this mask, thinking it will keep you safe. The mask is who you are. Or more appropriately, who you think you are.

The mask is the identity we create for ourselves on the outside. It is our "ego"—or our conscious mind, personified. The ego identity is who and what we think we are. And the ego identity is the self we show to others. Carl Jung, the famous Swiss psychiatrist and founder of analytical psychology, called this ego mask the "persona",

16

or the part of ourselves that we identity with and present to the world.

When we are operating from our ego identity, we put ourselves at the center of everything. We look at everything and others in relation to ourselves. How do others see me? Am I good enough? How do I measure up?

We spend a great deal of time proving to ourselves and to others how good, worthy, and special we are. We unconsciously or consciously aim to be as good as, or even to out dance others. Some of us may even want to take center stage in this masquerade ball we are all participating in and be the belle or the beau of the ball.

We may be looking for admiration and adoration. Perhaps on a deeper level, we are looking to be seen as loveable and worthy of love. We judge ourselves and others by how well we measure up. We turn an intense focus on perfecting our own performance. Personal worthiness, power, and success are largely dependent upon individual performance at this ball. Do I measure up to the standards? Do I exceed them? Is my mask and accompanying costume beautiful enough and worthy of accolades? Will I be invited to participate again? All of this will be determined by me and what I do. So, I turn my attention to myself, and see myself as the center of

17

the universe. I focus on how I look. How I sound. What I achieve. What others think of me. How much stuff I possess. I judge my interactions and my encounters in accordance to how they relate to me. In essence, I am the center of the entire universe, and everything that is happening is happening to me, for me, or because of me. My self-concept, self-identity, and self-esteem is dependent on how I behave, meet the standards I set for myself, and prove my worthiness.

To be able to participate in this grand masquerade ball, you must groom yourself and prepare for it carefully. Creating this identity mask takes years of work and focus. It has to fit properly, so you can wear it proudly and let it represent you to the outside world. You have to craft it meticulously.

Chapter 4

Masks Help Mold Your Identity

I am not knocking these ego masks. Carl Jung told us that these masks are, indeed, normal and necessary for our psychological personal survival in the world. How else can we take all the energy, conscious and unconscious, inside of our brains, channel it outward, and make our way in the world? It is a monumental task of survival and separation we embark on when we are born into this world.

What is going on inside our minds—all our own thoughts and feelings are silent to others. A large portion of our brain's functioning is unknown even to our own self. We contain multitudes inside of our brains that we know nothing about consciously. We are left to only sort out our conscious experience of all that is happening within us and to us, select what we want to present to others, and somehow make meaning of it. With this process, we also establish our autonomy and separateness.

Our individual ego identities are formed from this separateness. I am me and you are you. We are different. We are separate. If we weren't separate, how would we function? This separate identity is necessary. This mask

19

we wear is part of becoming who we are as an individual separate from others.

Wearing our masks, we cast ourselves as the protagonists and heroes of our own individual lives. In reality, these lives we create are merely scripts written from the stories we have learned from others. What those around us have taught us is what we emulate. Our parents, our upbringing, the culture we were born in, how we were socialized all play a role in helping us create what we think is our unique identity and subsequent ego mask. We adapt the scripts passed down to us and star in them and act as if they are original and that we had written them ourselves.

Performing in the center of what we think is our own universe, we get a false sense of being at the controls of our own lives.

As a result, we focus on creating a story line with our own survival, success, and in the best of circumstances, our own thriving happy ending. Our ego masks help us serve the character of ourselves well. A normal part of our developmental journey is the creation of this ego identity mask. It helps us navigate and function in the outside world. We need this mask in order to function as an individual in this world. Without it, we would flounder. Creating this mask is what we as humans do as part of our survival in the world.

These ego identity masks pose one danger, however. The danger is that we think the mask is all we are. We lose sight of the fact that the mask is only an outside cover of who we are. It is made up of our experiences and who we think we should be, along with how we want others to see us. It doesn't encompass the incredible depth and unconscious wisdom that lies within us. There is a vast part of ourselves that we aren't attuned to or even unaware of yet. If we totally tune out of and lose sight of this place and ignore it, we are not whole. We are merely a shell of ourselves. And something is always "off" within us.

This deeper place I refer to is what I call our "wise self". This wise self is connected to much more than just our outside or direct experience. It transcends anything we have been taught as rules or answers by others around us. The wise self that resides within us is connected to something greater than us—something that goes beyond just our own individual identity. It has resided within us all along, as a dormant sage that already knows what is most important. But this sage is not as concerned with day to day life, with being the best, or with competing

21

and proving. It knows our full potential as a human being and calls us to fulfill it. This wise self has other, bigger priorities. Priorities that may not fit neatly with the identity mask we have created or the stories others have told us. Since these priorities seem too big or don't fit with the ones we have created for ourselves, we reject this part of ourselves and drown it out.

As we spend our lives perfecting and polishing our masks and participating in the masquerade balls with others, we may occasionally experience what I call the wise self's whisperings coming from an inner portal where it resides. The portal I refer to is a point of access to the wiser self within us located deep beyond the mask. You see, our wise self is always trying to communicate with us. It is trying to get us to integrate it into our lives so that we fulfill our highest potential. It doesn't seek to destroy our security as we might fear it will. In fact, it is proud of what we have accomplished and learned and become so far. What it wants is for us to listen to it so that we can be true to the part of ourselves that is so much greater than the beautiful ego identity we have created for ourselves. It wants us to see ourselves as much bigger than that ego mask. It wants us to focus on contributing our gifts to the world each day in service of a calling that goes beyond the individual stories we have created in our daily lives. It calls us to see a bigger picture, to see our connectedness with others and all things, and to focus on what is truly important on a bigger scale.

This inner wisdom knows us. It is our deeper essence. It is a piece of us that wants to be heard and wants to help us change. It wants to teach us what we have yet to learn, and to turn us into teachers for others. Its whisperings have come to us in familiar forms over the years. Gnawing stabs in our stomachs. Sudden feelings of uneasiness and discontent.

When we sit alone, without filling our days with doing all the things we think we should do, without pursuing goals or material things—we can even feel them more strongly. Their sudden appearance out of what seems like nowhere, scares us. Maybe we aren't sure what we'll find if we go inside this whispering portal and listen. Everything we have created for ourselves is nice and neat and controlled within the ego identity of our mask. The whispers lead to an unexplored place inside of us that isn't as familiar as the story of ourselves we have so adeptly created. The unfamiliarity scares us. What might we find there? What might we have to change if we stop what we are doing and listen? What if what it is trying to tell us doesn't fit with what we are doing? What if our wise self sees us as much bigger than we think we are? Instead of trying to decipher the messages, we instead reactively block the portal. We fill the void that is there with more of what we already are good at doing.

We set more goals. We accumulate more material stuff that we can use as distracting chairs against a door that we don't want opened. We push the chairs against the portal and feel relieved. They are orderly and beautiful. All the goal achievement and the doing and the material stuff keeps us distracted and gives us a sense of control. We don't need to go inside the portal. Perhaps we are afraid of what we might find when we access our wise self in the portal. It is familiar yet foreign to us. It may disrupt what we have so neatly created on the outside.

It may ruin everything. We tell ourselves that we don't need to listen. If we ignore it, it will go away. Our ego mask identity is funny like that. It wants to protect us against everything. We become so dependent on it, we even let it protect us from our own wise self.

The Dilemma

As you go about your way in the world, the ego mask seems to suffice to get you what you think you need and want. But unless it is well informed and guided by your inner wise self, it is not fully you. Something is always missing from you. You are connected to much more than yourself. Your ego identity disconnects you from this universal source, where you are connected to everyone and everything else. It separates you, and in essence, makes you think that you are disconnected, unique, and different. The paradox here is that while you are different in the sense that you bring unique gifts and contributions to make to the world around you, you are also the same as everyone and everything else. You are made of the same fabric. You bleed when you are cut, as does every other living being on the planet. The 2020 pandemic illustrates that pretty profoundly. We all are fragile, human, and susceptible to the same fate. We are born and we die. Life does not differentiate any one of us. The fragility of life is the uniting force and larger universal law that presides over us all. The differences and distinctions we make among ourselves and the daily dramas of our lives are not present in the realm of our inner wise self. Our higher task after all these years of perfecting this outer ego mask identity is to learn to carefully dismantle it so that we can integrate the wisdom of our inner wise self into it, and live according to this universal law. We must destroy the identity we have created thus far in order to become our whole self. We must change how we have learned to see ourselves and our place in the world, and become more conscious about our everyday actions and choices. We must change from a fragmented version of ourselves to a whole, integrated one.

We resist this call to change because we are comfortable in our uniqueness. We have affiliated with what others expect us to be and have adapted quite well. We have created a nice neat life and feel a sense of control. Control is important to our equilibrium, safety, and sense of self. While there may be a pull to change—the pull to stay the same is just as great if not greater. We have built up an immunity to change that resists the pull.

"We must destroy the identity we have created thus far in order to become our whole self."

Chapter 5

Mask Construction Phase #1: Learning to Please

Let's talk about how you might have gone about constructing this persona you use as your mask identity. I'll share with you some highlights from the creation of my own mask over the years.

Building a mask identity starts early. I found myself feeling conflicted and torn at a young age between what I saw and felt in my inner world and what I was being taught and actually experiencing in the outer world. Like we all do, I had so many questions.

It was comforting to hear the answers, even if some of them really didn't make sense. They provided a semblance of security and a semblance of control. Because not knowing the answers, or the "truth", was really scary. Uncomfortable.

Disorienting. Anxiety provoking.

I was told and taught the "rules' of living, the meaning of life, why we were all here, and what we should aspire to in this lifetime. What was right and what was wrong. What was good and what was bad. What was acceptable and not acceptable. I was given the "answers"

27

that would help me survive, live, and thrive. Life's rule book, survival guide, and secrets to success all rolled into one. When I questioned the "rules" or poked holes in the logic of some of the answers I was being given, I was told that some things must just be believed with faith, even if they didn't make sense.

"Thomas the apostle doubted Jesus' validity, and look at the disastrous outcome of his doubt," I was warned as part of my Christian teachings.

The main message was that sometimes you just had to take truth for face value and believe it because that is what you were told. Doubt and questioning truth could only get you in trouble, or have you be ostracized by those who knew and believed the real truth and didn't question it. Doubt the answers, and you'd be viewed as bad. Disobedient. A non-believer. So, who had these answers? Well, all the responsible adults did, of course!

My parents were the first set of adults anointed by me as all-knowing truth keepers, because they fed me and took care of me and wanted me to be safe. And other family members and friends around us knew the right things as well, as did members of our community. The priest at the church we went to and the people there knew the answers, too. We talked about what the truth was a lot during services and at our religious celebrations. My teachers at school had the answers, and so did the politicians I watched on television and the doctors who tended to me when I was sick.

I just needed to ask.

There was never a shortage of answers to keep me comfortable and safe. There was no need for anxiety about uncertainty or not knowing. There was a ready-made answer for everything. There were ready-made rules for everything. Everything was just fine. The world was only a relatively safe place if you knew the right answers. If you knew what to do and what not to do.

There was a catch though. You had to believe the answers given from those who had them and obey the rules. You had to understand what was required of you. You had to be good. If you were bad, bad things would happen. You had to do what people who had the answers told you to do, and follow their examples and advice. It was pretty simple, really.

When something didn't seem right or make sense, it wasn't good to question or show it. Just agree. Behave. Put on the "good girl" mask and don't doubt the answers. This would please the adults that had the answers. This would keep you as safe as possible in this big, unknown world. It would help you be a normal insider, and not be seen as an oddball outsider. Pleasing others was important.

Wearing the pleasing mask kept you included and accepted. It kept you safe.

Chapter 6

Mask Construction Phase #2: Learning to Polish

At the age of 6, I realized that pleasing the rule-makers and merely believing the stories I was taught weren't sufficient enough to create a mask that was durable for all situations. I learned that I needed to keep adding more layers to it, to make it more suitable for the complexities of living.

As a child growing up in Athens, Greece, with a Greek mother and an American father, I was socialized in two different worlds. I attended an English-speaking, international school, yet was socialized in the Greek cultural norms as a by-product of living in the country.

As a toddler and young child, I looked different than most of the people around me. My naturally straight, long, blond hair, porcelain fair skin, and yellow-green eyes stood out from the predominantly dark, curly-haired, brown-eyed, olive-skinned features most children living in Athens had inherited. As a result of this physical difference, I received constant unsolicited admiration from strangers. People would regularly stop my mother on the street during our walks, pinch my cheek, and gush to us about how "cute" and "adorable" I looked. "She is a

31

living doll," was a common sentiment people of all ages would express to my mother. It was if I was seen as a pretty toy—a shell—and not a real live person. But it felt really good to be admired like that.

In our first-grade play about Greek mythology, the Greek language teacher cast me as Aphrodite, the goddess of love and beauty, because she thought I "fit the part." I resonated more with Athena, the goddess of wisdom, and objected to the casting.

"I want to be Athena," I asserted.

"My dear, Aphrodite is the goddess every girl wants to be. She was the most beautiful goddess," she assured me in a 'teacher knows best' voice. And she must know best, I told myself. She is the teacher. But deep inside, I knew that I resonated with the energy of Athena more than Aphrodite. I wasn't Aphrodite, no matter how I appeared to others.

The teacher just reinforced what I was experiencing— that admiration and adoration from others came automatically—just from looking beautiful in the eyes of those around me.

Then came second grade—and a big change occurred in this fragile and adored outside appearance of mine. I learned just how easily this unearned physical admiration and adoration can abruptly change to contempt, fear, and disgust. This unearned admiration I had unknowingly provoked was absolutely fragile and fickle.

My right eye suddenly developed what is referred to as a "lazy eye" condition. It is caused by a loose muscle in the eye, and the eyeballs stray from the middle of the eye, instead of staying centered. The muscle problem was quite severe and instead of being in the middle of my eye, my eyeball permanently stayed crossed off center, anchoring itself towards my nose. I could still see clearly but had to adjust the orientation of my vision, so I didn't trip over things right in front of me. Nothing had changed for me except for when I looked in the mirror my right eye was crossing inward and it was weird to look at.

Even though I felt no different, to others I must have looked dramatically different. I went from being adored and admired by others to being pointed at, taunted, and teased.

At school a ring of children gathered around me and chanted, "Look at the cross-eyed lion! Look at the ugly lion!"

This type of taunting didn't happen just once, and it wasn't coming from just a few bullies or "mean girls". I vividly remember drinking water from a water fountain one day and an upperclassman pushing my head down onto the porcelain fountain, laughing at me, saying, "I'm just helping you see the water better, since your eyes are crooked." My "best" friend stopped playing with me during recess and instead, joined in the taunting. She had been my playmate since day one of school, and we had shared secrets and played together on the swings. She was my friend. She said she liked me. And now, there she was—pointing at me and whispering to a new group of girls she was surrounded with. She went from smiling at me to laughing at me, just like everyone else at school suddenly seemed to do. All of this because of the way I looked. Because I looked different. Because I looked defective to many of them.

I didn't know why the sudden aversion happened or understand it. What I did know is how it felt to be shunned and ostracized for a physical difference that I had no control over. The isolation, despair, sadness, and devastation I felt as a result burned an iron brand imprint in my soul that is still warm to this day.

Medicine has a way of working miracles. Eight months later, I went into surgery to tighten the muscle and correct the lazy eye. After enduring months of recovery and donning eye patches to prevent infection and protect my constantly blood shot eye—it happened. I looked in the mirror and my eye was straight again. Back to normal. I wasn't different anymore! The bad nightmare had ended and things were the way they were before. The kids stopped teasing me. No one stopped and stared or pointed at my eyes anymore. It's as if an evil spell had been broken and everything had been transformed.

But there had been a dramatic change. I was no longer the same. I had added a big piece of imaginary fabric to my mask. How I looked on the outside mattered more to others than who I was on the inside. The mask needed to be pretty. I needed to add polish to the mask for it to look good to others.

Less Ego, More Soul

Chapter 7

Mask Construction Phase #3: Learning to Prove

Moving forward, middle school and high school were great times for me. I attended an English-speaking, international school in Athens, Greece. The kids that attended there were from twelve different countries—the common denominator for all was the English-speaking requirement. Many of their parents were in the foreign service or expatriates from the United States or other countries. Others, like myself, were children of military service members or government contractors stationed overseas.

I always loved to learn and books were like athletics to me. While gym class was something that I looked for any possible alibi to allow me to be excused from, I easily excelled in most academic subjects. I found writing and public speaking to be as natural as some of my peers found running or playing sports. Books were windows into vast hidden worlds just waiting to be discovered. And books were a gateway to questions—oh, so many questions! When I read, I felt like Pandora in Greek mythology. Being told not to open the jar containing secrets (or box in contemporary versions of the story)—but opening it anyway. Out popped all the scary and unexplainable things we, as a society, were trying so hard to contain or explain. Curiosity and wonder were double-edged swords; they opened up new worlds yet made us realize that the answers we seek are merely stories we had made up as explanations in that moment in time.

Writing and speaking were not only vehicles of self-expression, but also, of synthesizing seemingly disparate ideas and thoughts and finding unity among them. They provided a portal to access and tap into a much deeper place inside. The innate power and wisdom found inside that portal could flow through and reach people in a deeper place, going well beyond the tight confines of the collective masks we were wearing. It allowed, if only temporarily, the transcendence from external differences and divisions to a common place inside us that relates to a deeper human experience on the planet.

This natural connection to a deeper portal helped me see a peek behind the masks other people were wearing. I could sense and feel their deeper hopes and struggles and connect and empathize with even those who were not like me. Others considered me popular as a result. I was liked and admired. But this time it wasn't because of how I looked. I was popular because I was tapping into a place behind the collective masks and courageously showing others what I saw through my acceptance and admiration of their inner gifts.

A new part of my mask identity came under construction as a result of the passage of dating.

Costume Parade of Young Romance and Perfection

As a junior in high school, I was smitten with a boy. We became inseparable. I told myself that this is what love is, and that every love story that I had ever read had led me to the experience of this relationship. I projected every idealized version of what love was supposed to be like onto this one, in my eyes at the time, gloriously perfect person. Yet despite the stories that I had created about love, I know now that no one, myself included, can ever live up to a romanticized ideal of perfection. We are not perfect humans. But at the time, I wasn't mature enough to understand that. Instead, I focused on a different facet that struck at the fragile foundation of the relationship. His parents were well-educated, upper middle-class Greeks. When they realized that the relationship was blossoming and moving into the college years, their questions began to mount.

"What do her parents do?"

Less Ego, More Soul

"Where did they go to school?"

A virtual pedigree background check commenced. While I had met his parents and I was well-known in the school, this was now getting too close for comfort for their liking at the time. Understandably so. We were so young. But most important at the time was not who I was and what I stood for. Perhaps they thought I was too young to have yet developed a concrete sense of self. The questions that were most important for the screening were not about me at all, though. They were about what was around me.

Was my socio-economic background and pedigree up to par? Did I meet the unwritten requirements they had about where and by whom the serious girlfriend or future wife of their only son was raised? Was there sufficient social status and standing in my upbringing?

When he told me that his parents had these sort of questions, I naively gave the real answers. My parents both came from very poor families. My mother got married just a few years out of high school and had me shortly thereafter. My dad was in the enlisted ranks in the Air Force, as he saw that as his only ticket to get out of the small town he was raised in and a way to pay for an education. My mother was a homemaker, and spent her days attending to the house and raising her two daughters. My dad was a hard worker who even worked two jobs for a period of time with hopes to provide his family with more things and opportunity than he had while growing up.

I guess my story didn't quite measure up, as my boyfriend told me he was going to continue dating me despite what his parents thought. I was puzzled but more than that, I felt shame. Shame on me for not measuring up. Shame on me for not being good enough. I would have to do better. I would have to prove to them and to him that I was smart and successful. I would prove it by achieving more than others. Then I would pass the test and be accepted, wouldn't I?

I added a new piece to my mask—*proving*.

As an epilogue to this story, I broke up with him a year later. But the proving piece of the mask had already been sturdily constructed.

Less Ego, More Soul

Chapter 8

The Masquerade Ball

As an adult, my ego mask was well formed. It was sturdy and a beautifully designed and well-made masterpiece. While I viewed myself as my own person, I followed many of the rules and conventions I was socialized with in contemporary society, and made sure I was a dutiful daughter, citizen, church member, and wife. I created a story with myself starring successfully in it, doing my best to meet and exceed the expectations I had painstakingly created for myself in the script called "My Life".

I tried hard to be that good girl. I polished my exterior. I collected formal education and certifications. I received accolades for my performance at work. I could please, polish, and prove with the best of them. I was proud of who I had managed to become. There were parts of my identity that I chose for myself as well. Not all of it was from the influences around me. But for the most part, I excelled at adapting to the norms around me and achieving according to the rules prescribed by conventional standards.

Less Ego, More Soul

As a result of this successful adaptation and much hard work, I was admitted to attend fine masquerade balls, where the parade of masks was on full display, showing them all in their hand-made, magnificently crafted glory.

There were the status masks, branded with designer names emblazoned across the front of them, shouting, "I am important."

There were the quiet, mysterious masks, intricately designed for hiding and going incognito.

There were the name-dropping masks that bore photos of famous people all over them, evoking admiration and attention for their importance.

There were masks made of ice, feigning a cool exterior designed to prevent emotion from escaping from the cracks.

There were the expert masks.

There were the forever-young masks, with overly-plumped lips and pulled rubber band-stretched skin, desperately hiding any sign of aging and furiously fighting for fleeting youth.

Less Ego, More Soul

They were all amazing masks. The parades were spectacular—brilliantly orchestrated for a phenomenal show. And yet, despite the preparation and careful display, there was something eerie about these galas. The eyes.

If you looked carefully into the eyes not covered by the mask, you could see into them. It's as if people's eyes could not be masked. They led to that portal I could so adeptly access in high school. The portal that transcended us into oneness—and made every mask at the ball melt away. I could see behind the pomp and circumstance at the ball. I could get a glimpse of the person's wise self behind the mask. The glimpse was brief and fleeting—but it was real. I knew it was there.

Mask Musings: Self-Reflection

Over the course of your life, you have built your own ego identity mask. It is the self you identify with on the outside and the self you present to the world. It includes your worldly accomplishments, all that you have achieved, what you have learned so far, and the mechanisms you have created to ensure your psychological survival as a separate human. Your ego identity mask is who you think you are on the outside and the image you portray to others.

Take a few moments as you reflect on what I just described as some key events that influenced parts of my own ego mask identity creation. Think about your own.

Jot down the answers to the following questions:

1. What part of me wants to please others?

2. How did I learn to do that?

3. What does being "good" mean to me?

4. What am I doing when I am pleasing?

5. What questions do I reject or dismiss because they may displease others?

6. What part of me is focused on image, outer appearance, and how I look?

7. When did I feel and learn the importance of outside polish?

8. What do I do to prove my worthiness to myself? To others?

9. How do I define success in my life?

10. What outer standards do I use to measure my success and the success of others?

11. What material things or status symbols do I use as indicators?

12. What parts of myself have I trained myself to hide because I fear rejection or ridicule from others?

13. What innate strengths have I owned and capitalized on?

14. What conventional standards of living have I adapted as the definition of normal?

PART II. THUNDERBOLTS

Less Ego, More Soul

Chapter 9

The Call to Change

This ego mask you come to identify with and the conventional life you create works well for a while. It may feel like you have everything under control. Until something happens to turn it all upside down. It is the moment in your life when a thunderbolt out of the sky suddenly strikes you without warning. It shakes you to the core and knocks you off your feet.

This force disorients you, but also knocks away the many layers of false identity you have spent years so adeptly creating. It shakes your understanding of the diverse stories you have learned from others about what is true and important. It opens up that musty, covered place inside of you that you have stacked up chairs of distraction against for years, in a desperate attempt to block its whispers.

When this thunderbolt strikes you, those chairs you secured against the imaginary door are completely knocked over. As a result, a pathway to those ignored inner whisperings is blown open and painfully revealed.

This powerful thunderbolt can come in different forms:

- The sudden death of a loved one.
- News of our own illness or close call with death.
- A divorce or end of an intimate relationship.
- An unanticipated loss of our job.
- Something totally unexpected that appears out of nowhere and threatens and assaults our health, well-being, or livelihood.

No amount of problem-solving or goal setting or achieving or tightening control can help you regain your footing when a thunderbolt strikes. Stories you have created about yourself and the world and all the things you have become good at doing offer you no protection from the force of the thunderbolt. You are left vulnerable and exposed, without clear answers to anything. Nothing makes sense anymore. You are struck down with a jolting electric shock and are forced to fall to your knees.

In this vulnerable, fully exposed place, you begin to question everything you thought you had previously figured out. You question everything about your own identity and behavior. The simple answers you had believed to be true about basic things in life and the world no longer seem relevant or sufficient. Everything you thought you had already neatly figured out and was neatly managed and controlled has now been turned around for re-examination. You feel off kilter, ungrounded, and disoriented since you are now re-evaluating the myriad of choices you have made over the years and wondering if they align with what you truly find to be important.

When this thunderbolt strikes:

- You are forced to tear off the mask you have created as your ego identity over the years and look much more deeply inside yourself.
- You question who you think you are in contrast to who you really are.
- You realize that the sense of true fulfillment in your life goes beyond your own individual goal achievement, fame, or fortune.
- Things you previously defined as measures and markers of success no longer seem relevant or resonant.
- You start to realize that you are not the center of the universe and are part of something much bigger than the small scenes of your own individual life.
- You are called to change.

While I have experienced this thunderbolt aftermath personally, I know that I am not alone. Over the years in my work with thousands of highly successful achievers, I have heard countless stories of these thunderbolt experiences. One after the other, people have recounted descriptions of these thunderbolts striking head on, followed by deep soul searching for meaning and life transformation in the aftermath.

One such experience is vividly imprinted in my mind from a successful mid-level executive I encountered. She had been promoted into her current role about two years earlier, and as we talked, I was overwhelmed by the power of her presence. By that, I mean by her grounded, calm, authentic, almost Zen-like demeanor, deep listening skills, and unusual level of self-awareness. The results of a survey given to the employees that worked directly for her were some of the highest scores I had seen. The feedback on a survey about her leadership effectiveness was unanimously positive, describing her as one of the best leaders most of the respondents had ever interacted with.

When I asked her what she attributed this positive reaction to her leadership to, she told me her thunderbolt story. She had been diagnosed with a life-threatening brain tumor at the age of 42, six years prior to our current conversation. While a successful surgery to remove it had eliminated the dire threat to her life and brought her back to health, she recounted how that experience had changed her forever. She described the feelings of intense anguish she felt when she had received the diagnosis, and how the months leading up to her surgery and subsequent healing and fear of recurrence caused her to go inward and do a complete self-evaluation of herself and her life up until then.

"When you are faced with dying, it makes you become more committed to what you want living to look like," I remember her saying. "It made me re-evaluate all the unimportant things I was involved in, who I was being, and in the end—what I wanted my life to stand for."

She added: "The things that bothered me or that I worried about before my diagnosis are just not important. I am on a different mission because of that experience. It is very hard to rattle me or move me off that new course, and I am less afraid of expressing myself. I am forever changed to the core."

The common denominator in her and others' thunderbolt experiences was that they struck

unexpectedly out of nowhere, causing a screeching halt
to business and life as usual. They threatened all sense of
comfort and control and created a major upheaval in the
routines of their lives. They struck hard, through the core,
and cracked the ego identity mask the person associated
with identity. The thunderbolt aftermath forced an
examination of who and what they fundamentally
identified with at a deeper level, beyond the identity they
projected and thought was real. It provoked them to
reject the outside image ego mask identity they had so
aptly created and question everything they had so neatly
identified with all these years.

This fallout made them reacquaint themselves with
that familiar internal place that had made contact with
them long ago. That inner voice, that place of knowing,
whispered and spoke in code. This voice was a wise self
they knew was there, but that they were so out of touch
with. This voice was not out of touch with them, though.
It was connected to them and to everything. Most
important, it was sitting right there all along. Right in the
seat of their souls.

This post-thunderbolt time they described was an
incredibly disorienting period to most. It was described

as a time of overwhelming fear and uncertainty. Of ungrounded lack of clarity or direction.

Years of rationalizing, denying, and being out of alignment with their inner voice of wisdom came into full display. They could no longer ignore that disconnect they had felt. The thunderbolt made them face it head-on. It attacked head-on the immunity to change they had built up.

It made them question who they were, what they wanted, what was important, and what was most meaningful. It was a time described to me as a painful realization that what they had spent their time up until then chasing and doing was not what necessarily brought them true fulfillment and connection. That going after more goal achievement, money, and material things would no longer work for them as identifiers of success. Nor would listening to what the conventional authorities were telling them they should want. It was an upheaval of massive proportions that they had no roadmap for.

It was also incredibly painful to have their entire being broken open—as if an unidentified internal organ had suddenly been taken out of their bodies and was lying vulnerably without cover. It had to be handled gently and carefully and placed in a place that would protect its fragility while being examined thoroughly.

This exposure had brought them face to face with someone inside of themselves that they on one level, knew intuitively, yet had not gotten to know and trust consistently or intimately. A part of themselves that was always there, yet not frequently connected to or honored by their day-to-day ego mask identity, or by the neat life they had built.

It was their wise self. Wise woman, wise man, whatever face you want to ascribe to it.

You may know this part of yourself. You have a wise self that resides inside of you.

This wise self is your own internal wisdom that is connected to a universal wisdom greater than the individual self you see as your outer identity. This wise self is not your current name, where you grew up, who your parents are, what race or gender you identify with, or what you do for a living. Whatever you choose to call it, there is a place inside of yourself that is uniquely you yet connected to everything around you. It doesn't matter how you explain it or label it.

This is the place that will ground you after a thunderbolt strikes. This is the person you must get reacquainted with more intimately. This is the person that you already know—yet have lost touch with. This is the voice you so often ignored. This is the voice you must finally pay attention to. This is the voice that will help you become whole.

Hiding and Seeking

I have had several thunderbolts in my life. Their force was overwhelming, and they provoked so many questions and inner soul searching. They forced me to go inside and meet my wise self and listen to her. I had had whisperings and many glimpses of her throughout my life. I also followed some of her guidance without knowing where it was coming from. But the mask identity was stronger than her gentle whispers, and it often overruled her counsel. Integrating her into my own ego identity was and still is an ongoing process.

When I was 35 years old, I was considered as relatively successful by the conventional standards many used to look from the outside in at me. I held an executive-level job in a large Fortune 200 company and had surpassed the six-figure salary success threshold I had set for myself a decade earlier. I had accumulated several formal degrees from educational institutions and collected numerous certifications in my field. I was married and had a house in a nice suburban neighborhood in Northern Virginia. I worked hard and pushed myself to the max.

I had ambitions to climb to the highest echelons in the corporate leadership chains in my field and heralded the next title as my moving target of success. My identity was pretty well-defined, and my mask portrayed it.

My body was a constant messenger from the inner portal to my wise self, warning me to examine the deeper voice behind the mask. My chronic headaches caused by undetected stress were the first signs of this attempt at communication. While I conveyed outwardly that I loved my job and this corporate climb is what I wanted, something felt off at a deeper level. While part of my job at the time tapped into the speaking, writing, learning, connecting with people, and teaching—all that I discovered as natural callings in high school—much of it did not. When I was immersed in the part of the job that transcended my mask identity, it didn't feel like a job, but as something I was being called from somewhere to bring forward. The other things that I had gotten so good at over the years were not as meaningful to me.

Approximately 80 percent of my daily effort was spent on the mask identity parts of my job—pleasing, polishing, and proving.

According to the National Institute of Mental Health, stress signals to our bodies that we are in danger. Biologically, our brain is wired to help us survive and protect us from that danger. In the past, that danger would present itself as being "eaten by a wild animal in the jungle". Our nervous systems would go into automatic mode, since the time it takes to ponder the situation with rational thinking could mean life or death—literally being eaten by a tiger. Our stress response includes the release of hormones that increase our heart rate and blood pressure, slow our digestion, and tense our muscles. This quick response provides readiness of our physical resources to either engage in a fight or run as fast as we possibly can to survive the wild animal attack—or what we call the "fight or flight" mode.

The problem is that our brain doesn't distinguish the life and death aspect of the situation. It recognizes when we perceive threat—any threat—even the threat of failure or agitation, the same way it does physical danger. When we are experiencing a situation that promotes mental anxiety or stress, our bodies exhibit the same physical lifesaving response.

Over time, continued strain on your body from stress may contribute to serious health problems, such as heart disease, high blood pressure, diabetes, and other illnesses, including mental disorders such depression or anxiety. And as we know from multiple research studies, those conditions are dangerous to our physical health and can eventually lead to the ultimate consequence: death.

When I ignored my headaches, the breathing issues started. "Anxiety" was the official label I was given for my sudden gasps for air, and the seemingly inability to breathe that struck without warning.

"Look inside," the portal was pleading. "I am here. I know what you need."

I distracted myself from the voice by doing more. More proving. More polishing. The more I tightened the mask, the louder my body pushed back. My wise woman was a persistent one at that. Extra strength Tylenol and meditation exercises helped me keep the constant pushing under management and control. The tighter my neck and shoulder muscles tensed, the more tightly under control everything was.

Until the thunderbolt hit from out of nowhere. It was a tricky thunderbolt, since it didn't hit me directly. It hit my father.

It was the eve of my father's 60th birthday. He had just retired from the nine-to-five job world a few months earlier and was busy mapping out the possibilities for his next act. Then it struck.

That tricky cold and cough he had been wrestling with all summer wasn't a cold after all. It was a cancerous tumor on his left lung. The doctor had rattled off a spattering of statistics for life expectancy in his condition and provided a grim prediction: he had six more months of life to live, maximum.

While this book is not intended to be a memoir or a story about my parents, I couldn't write it without drawing upon the thunderbolt experience given to me from my dad's own life and sudden death sentence.

As one of seven children of a farmer struggling to make ends meet in a small, rural town in Tennessee, my dad had found the military a perfect escape route from what he believed were his limited options for the future. The story he latched onto was a clear and clean opportunity in his mind—joining the military would allow him to serve his country, see the world, attend college fully funded by Uncle Sam, go to law school, retire by age forty and then start a new career as a lawyer. A pretty well-thought out plan for an 18-year old farm boy from rural Tennessee with no money or connections. He harbored a secret, idealized childhood dream of arguing trial cases and defending innocent people with limited means in court.

He joined the armed forces as part of the enlisted ranks in the military class system right after graduating from high school. Four years later, he ended up with an assignment in Athens, Greece as a young airman in the Air Force. It was a long way from the rural towns he had been raised in, or from the very few places he had ever been for that matter. Although it was already his second foray overseas since joining the military, Greece was different. To him, Athens summoned visions of an ancient, exotic locale yet felt strangely familiar to him when he arrived there.

Athens was a smoggy, bustling city built underneath the majestic, towering ruins of a nearly 2,500-year-old religious temple. It literally looked like a place God would live in, with its regal marble columns and intricately carved statues emerging from the sky and perched on a hill above the city, visible from all directions.

Just as his young idealistic imagination would have envisioned it, it was in this city that he would meet his version of a Greek goddess. He first encountered her not in the heavens, but at a party. A fellow service member had met and married a local Greek woman and was hosting a celebration of their nuptials at his new home. Among the invitees was my mother, a barely 20-year old former high school classmate and friend of the bride's. She was extremely feminine and shy, with a reserved and demure demeanor.

My mother's own physical beauty—her Venusian, shapely figure and finely chiseled facial features gave her an ethereal, almost angelic quality. While others definitely noticed her beauty, she didn't have the confidence one would expect of a beautiful woman. The insecurities and social inequities she felt as a result of being the daughter of a poor, widowed housekeeper were rampant and imprinted deep in her psyche.

She was instantly smitten by my dad's quick and friendly smile, twinkling green eyes that squinted when he laughed, and sharply starched short-sleeved shirts that made him look like a movie star plucked right out of the

American cinema. He was thin and handsome, clean-cut, incredibly funny, easy to talk to, and disarmingly simple—unlike many of the boys she had encountered in Greece. He didn't seem to care who her parents were, where she lived, or what type of "dowry" she had. He was oblivious of class distinctions and took her for who she was at face value. He didn't care what her parents did for a living or whether or not she was going to college.

He was enamored by her aura, her simplicity, and her pure femininity. To him, she was the goddess of his dreams. And oh, how he looked at her! It was as if no other woman existed on the planet. He drove her around in his big American car, so flashy and unlike the compact European cars all the Greeks drove. He made her laugh so much, and she listened intently as he talked about his plans for the future. They both felt comfortable with each other—a familiarity that seemed to cross time and space. It was as if they were destined to find each other across continents at this very point in time and fall in love. Not even two months had passed and both smitten and hopelessly enamored with each other, they were engaged.

Three months later, they were married and my mother was pregnant with yours truly. Just like that—unplanned, unexpected, and quite unnerving—they were married and

66

soon-to-be parents. Two very young people at the cusp of adulthood, still unsure of their own identities, wrought with their own insecurities and family baggage, and still at the start of their own relationship, were faced with the responsibility of raising another life together.

The responsibilities of supporting and raising a family took over, as did the stories about what happiness should be. My dad built his mask with a predominate template of pleasing—following the stories others had laid out of what success should look like. He adhered to the norms set out for him by others, and tried his best he knew how to meet the expectations and responsibilities of family life.

He waited until he was about to retire, at the age of 60, to do some deeper soul searching about who he was and what was calling him. Right there, right when he finally began to look behind the mask he had so adeptly created to search for the answers, he was given a death sentence.

He died two years later.

The thunderbolt that hit me during his illness and subsequent death was splitting. It was as if I had been electrocuted so strongly that the charge vibrated throughout my entire being. Its force tore off my mask and challenged the identity I had created up until then.

I think the most electrifying realization was coming to terms of how fragile life is, and that our time on this earth is limited and precious. Too limited and precious to go through it without tapping into the deeper voice that was speaking to me and yet, I so adeptly ignored. Too short to go about it another day wearing and identifying with an outer identity mask that was built by me, for me, but didn't really fit me completely. It was way too small.

Masks are just coverings. They seek to hide us. I didn't want to be hidden any longer.

Chapter 10

Aftermath

Thunderbolts have a way of cracking open this inner portal I keep referring to and forcing us to look inside it. It wasn't just grief of losing a parent that was the catalyst—it was the grief of a life not fully lived. Of missing a big piece of myself that I knew was calling me to something deeper. Of wasting time. It was the grief of not answering the constant and gnawing call to change.

I was left with no other choice but to look behind the torn mask and dive into the power portal summoning me. I needed to find the wise woman inside me that knew what I needed. The one I had ignored so often yet was always there waiting for me to find her. I'd like to say this process was filled with bright lights and trumpets blasting—and I suddenly was given an enlightened revelation. It was nothing like that. At first, it was like a numbness. As if time had stood still and nothing meant what it did before. It was as if the nerve endings in my body were frozen in place. Nothing moved.

Then there was despair. Where was she? Wasn't she supposed to give me the answers? Wasn't she supposed to come out and tell me what to do now?

I couldn't hear anything. Maybe she wasn't really there.

Then came a period of learning to just be still and listen without looking for or expecting a specific, defined outcome. That was really hard for me. It was as if I was reattaching a universally connected limb that had been quasi-separated from my body. There was a slow reconnection process that now had to take place; an integration of a piece of myself that had been so badly neglected by the domination of the individual identity mask. The wise woman had to reconnect with me slowly, through the portal. She wasn't there to annihilate the mask. She wanted to take her rightful place as a primary guide and advisor. The mask was a covering and a face— and had been created as a separate identity—away from her. She wanted me to include her. She wanted me to use her to make me whole.

To find her, I needed to learn to be patient. To wait. I needed to learn how to wait without doing or solving anything.

It wasn't an easy exercise, since my ego identity was so used to solving problems and taking quick, decisive and directed action. I followed my instincts and was directed to focus my attention on my senses.

70

Less Ego, More Soul

I took time off from work and took long walks. I lay on the bed and listened to soft music with my eyes closed. I took warm baths and lit soft candles and just sat there and listened. I wrote what I was feeling and thinking in a journal each day—and the words flowed through me without effort. I didn't know what I was writing. I just wrote. No answers flowed through the portal. Instead, the opposite happened. I was flooded with the questions. Oh, those haunting questions! Who am I? Why am I here? What does everything mean? Am I doing what I came here to do? Am I being who I came here to be? Am I leading a meaningful and fulfilling life? I had to sit still with the questions. I had to first listen and not jump to solving a problem or fixing everything. There was nothing to fix. I had to seek and find. I had to decide what to let go of. I had to understand what no longer fit. Then I had to learn to stay grounded and connected at this deeper level that wasn't dependent on my ego identity. Only then could I move forward and access and use my wise woman to serve in my own life and in the world.

It was a process. It took time. It took self-reflection, self-evaluation, and listening. For me, that unfolded with long walks in nature. I spent hours just staring at the ocean and watching the pelicans dance in unison over my head. I became drunk on the bubbles the waves spouted as they crashed open on the rocks engulfing the cliffs. I bore witness to the sun's magnificence as a brilliant ball of fire, lowering over the horizon to rest the potency of its flames each evening without extinguishing its power. I just observed it all with a new sense of awe. I would lie on my bed and feel my breath going in and out. Just breathing. Doing nothing—just feeling my own presence and depth of my being…fully.

And there was bypassing my logical, rational mind and tapping into my own creativity and unconscious mind through writing, drawing, and visualization exercises. I learned to decipher the language and the messages from my wise woman inside. The answers started to pour out of me, in code, mind you—but they were all there, clear as daylight.

Through accessing and listening to the wise woman, I changed.

Not just a simple, outward change, but a transformative internal change. My internal focus, decision-making, words, and actions transformed. So did how I thought about things. It was as if I had the same computer but was running it on an updated operating system. I looked the same, but the way I was operating was fundamentally different. I had been rebooted. I had a new anchor that was grounded. I could still wear a mask to navigate some of the intricacies of the outside world, but it was a transparent one. I could still see my wise woman behind it. It was as if the wise woman was now integrated into everything I did and all the decisions I made.

The mask and the wise woman were now speaking to one another and had an understanding and respect for each other. They were one whole—and we were all living in the same house.

Through these guided soul search sessions, I had learned how to listen to and be guided by my inner wise woman. She was there with what I needed all along. I just had to learn to find her and listen.

As someone who has studied human development and worked with people on their own personal growth most of my adult life, I have quite a bit of research knowledge and practical experience on this topic. I know a host of theories, have read hundreds of books, and have listened to thousands of people recount their unique experiences to me. What I am convinced of, as a result, is that this continual process of integration cannot be accomplished by reading a book or even a dozen books. It isn't about acquiring more or new knowledge. This process of learning to integrate your wise self into the prioritization and decision-making of your life can only be accomplished by going inside of yourself. It takes profound self-reflection, introspection, and a willingness to be uncomfortable with not having a clear-cut path forward. It takes surrender to the not knowing in order to trust in your own deeper knowing.

Chapter 11

A Disorienting Place for All of Us

As of this writing, in the Spring of 2020, you and I have been hit with a gargantuan thunderbolt impacting everyone around the world. We are experiencing a global health crisis, a pandemic that came out of nowhere and is impacting everyone. Most of the world is in some sort of stay-at-home quarantine period due to this crisis. We cannot comfortably and freely leave our houses due to the high risk of getting sick or spreading the illness, except to get food or medicine or attend to absolutely essential business. We wear masks when we do venture out for essentials, or if we are still going to a workplace that is considered "essential" during these times. Many of us are sick with this unfamiliar virus that is spreading. Some of us are hospitalized; some are even in critical condition. An unexpected number of us are eventually dying from this threatening organism.

Who could have predicted that the year of 2020 would bring this sudden, cataclysmic upset to our daily lives?

Everything "non-essential" has halted as we are ordered to stay inside the safety of our own homes to avoid continued spread of this invisible virus moving stealthily and steadily among us all.

Millions are filing for unemployment as their financial livelihoods have been severely impacted by the shutdowns.

I had no idea that this notion of a thunderbolt experience and subsequent soul searching I was writing about would become so relevant. I never thought that we would be hit by a massive, global thunderbolt of unprecedented proportions. That it would strike so suddenly and shake us to the very core of our beings.

You may be now sitting back during this thunderbolt experience and facing questions that are bubbling up in the midst and resulting aftermath. You may be having an identity crisis of some sorts as you are brought face to face with your own fragility as a human—and the fragility of those around you. You may be wondering if what you thought was important before all of this is really that important. You may also be questioning your own choices and behaviors.

Your wise self may have been thrust forward and your ego identity mask has been cracked. Your wise self may be speaking much more loudly now than that muffled whisper when your mask was securely in place.

Those designer handbags you covet and display as status symbols may feel pretty unimportant to you. Being impressed by people's titles and their social status may seem superficial and unaligned to your deeper sense of values. You watch people show sides of themselves that involve compassion, empathy, and kindness. None of these attributes you admire and resonate with in these moments have anything to do with material wealth, social status, goal achievement, fame, or other measures of success you may have become accustomed to using as metrics to judge yourself and others over the years. You may be embarrassed when you are faced with what might appear to you to be the shallowness your own surface identity. Yes, yours. That superficiality that you could perhaps spot in others but didn't see in your own self. The things that impressed you that really were meaningless but were prescribed to you as important from those around you or from the conventional thinking you were socialized with—and had become your own.

This self-evaluation can be a scary, disorienting place to be. It makes you challenge and question what felt neatly normal and in order throughout your life. Yet it is

77

also a time of renewal. An opportunity to discard the stories that no longer resonate with you or make sense. Maybe they never made sense, but you didn't stop to question. You didn't stop to go deeper and listen.

Maybe the aftermath of an event like a pandemic isn't a strong enough jolt to cause you to do this sort of complete reset and re-evaluation. Perhaps a different thunderbolt like the ones I mentioned earlier have shaken you to the core instead. Perhaps you have lost your job. Maybe you have lost a loved one or ended a relationship. Whatever the case, regardless of what kind of thunderbolt you have been hit with, I believe it is time for us all to wake us up to our deeper, wiser selves. That yearning for something more that you feel deep down from your core has always been trying to get your attention. It has been calling you. The thunderbolt experience just serves to knock your ego identity upside down and aside so that you have no choice but to listen. You are no longer immune to change.

Simple questions may be coming up for you as you've experienced this total loss of control and a staunch recognition of the commonality and fragility of all of humanity. Now is the time to reconnect to that neglected place and learn to listen to the deeper, wiser self that resides inside of you, that knows exactly what you need. It is time to find your wise self and come back full circle. It is time to become whole.

Thunderbolt Wake-up Call: Self-Reflection

1. Upon your last thunderbolt, whether the pandemic or something else, did you take time to reflect on the situation and dig around for your feelings?

2. Is the person you are being on a daily basis really the person you are or want to be at a deeper level?

3. What actions do you take on a regular basis that are not consistent with what you truly value?

4. Do you love, admire, respect the same things as before?

5. Are you focused on the right things for your wellbeing?

Less Ego, More Soul

PART III. GUIDED SOUL SEARCH SESSIONS

Less Ego, More Soul

Chapter 12

Homecoming: The Ultimate Discovery

While you were busy creating and wearing that outside ego identity and neatly organized life of yours, your inner wise woman was always there. Your wise self was trying hard to communicate with you and get you to listen and focus. While it may have gotten through on occasion, the chair you so desperately placed in front of it to block it out was pretty adept at keeping it from coming through too loudly and disrupting your neatly laid out goals and life plan. You were following a conventional guidebook laid out for you by others around you. Definitions of success and who you were based on how you were socialized and the stories you were taught about what was important and true. And you felt good about what you were creating—it kept you safe and feeling some sense of control.

Thunderbolts knock away that false sense of control and safety you have spent years creating.

Your mind may suddenly be in distress. The questions are flooding in, and that safety net you had created so diligently is no longer securely in place to provide the neatly organized answers that kept you in control. It

83

doesn't offer the level of protection you designed it for. You feel ungrounded, off kilter, and unsettled. Where are the answers? Just like Pandora in Greek mythology, the jar you dared not open has been open by the thunderbolt, and now cannot contain the things that are coming out of it. Even if you tried, you cannot put the lid back on.

You don't have the answers to the questions that are pouring through you. The things you thought were important may even seem meaningless or insignificant now. Those answers given to you from your parents, the people around you, the culture you grew up in, and the society around that kept you safe no longer suffice. They are too small, too incomplete to provide you comfort now. The uncertainty and discomfort you experience has surpassed the simple stories designed and carefully selected to soothe your discomfort. You must find another way to soothe the anxiety that arises from this new place of not knowing.

You now know that you must find a new way to know what you thought you already knew.

But how?

The place you are in is actually a gateway of great power, if you can surrender to not knowing and learn to

84

look inside. It leads to part of yourself that has a deeper knowing than anything you had been seeking on the outside. It has always been there with you and can always be accessed. The problem with it is that it may not speak the direct, immediate language you are used to speaking. It doesn't give you a clear-cut, daily roadmap. It doesn't fit into the designed, step-by-step, paint-by-numbers existence you have grown to prefer.

You need to learn how to access this portal and the wise part of yourself that resides there.

If you find yourself faced with a re-evaluation of yourself and your life as a result of a thunderbolt experience or from your deeper call to change, this book can help. It can help you tap into your wise self and begin to do the self-reflection needed to live and lead more in alignment with what is truly important to you.

These Guided Soul Search Sessions can help you learn how to tap into your own inner wisdom and re-create yourself. They will prod you to define what your deeper calling is, what is most important, and who you really are behind the ego identity mask you have learned to wear. More importantly, they will help you think and act more intentionally about the choices you make every single moment, and make sure that those choices are in alignment. They will ask you to make a deeper commitment to your whole self, and to live, contribute, and serve by the values you espouse to be important.

These Guided Soul Search Sessions that follow consist of three self-directed sessions over three weeks…just 21 days.

These weekly sessions will enable you to learn to survive and thrive without the need to please, prove, or project an impressive image in order to feel worthy and successful. They will help you reject the conventional stories you have learned to rely upon as your own reality. They will free you to be more truly connected to a deeper, wiser place inside you that isn't reliant on outside validation or approval.

The pages that follow do not provide a clear roadmap. They are not a prescribed method that involve goal setting and subsequent guaranteed results. While you may have learned to do that well over the years and are proud of your super-achiever ability to make things happen, your wise self isn't accessed that way. You will need to learn a new way to work and communicate with yourself. You will need to learn to go deep inside, listen, and wait. You will need to reject and let go of some of the old notions and stories that your mind is used to relying on. You will need to take some time and be patient. Instant oatmeal in a microwave is not what you will get here! When you learn to pause, listen, and be patient with yourself without trying to control, you will slowly but surely realize that you can no longer operate the way you have been operating thus far. What worked for you in the past is not what will work to keep you grounded and connected to your inner wise self.

You will be called to change.

For the next three weeks, you will spend time going through the three Guided Soul Search Sessions. Give yourself one week for each section.

Each week consists of an exercise that builds upon the other. Think of it as an excavation into a buried place inside of you. Each session gets you closer to uncovering that place. Here's an overview of what you will do:

Week #1: Embrace Yourself

This week, you will think about who you are and who you have become up until now. You will create a life's journey timeline depicting your experiences and what you have learned. You will answer a battery of targeted questions to allow you to really understand and recognize your own motivations, strengths, and attitudes and how they have been shaped over time.

Week #2: Find Your Inner Wise Woman

This week will be the most uncomfortable because there isn't a tangible product to point to. This is the week you spend time tuning into the inner voice—the voice of the wise woman that is you. You will be provided numerous options of how to do this, including a powerful visualization tool and a host of probing questions. The bulk of this session consists of listening and introspection.

Week #3: Create Your Personal Manifesto

The third week culminates with the creation of your own personal manifesto. This session allows you to integrate the voice of your wise woman into a declaration of who you are, what you believe, and what you are committed to. It is the creation of a decision-making and alignment tool for the actions of not the person you are now—but of the person you are becoming.

As you go through the three Guided Soul Search Sessions, pay attention to what you are feeling, thinking, and experiencing. Move beyond your discomfort with what you may be feeling. Let yourself fully immerse in each one. Put aside your tendency to want to rush back to "normal" and keep busy. These habits you have become accustomed to serve to distract you from the questions that emerge from your wise self and make you uncomfortable. Give yourself three weeks. Spend some dedicated time each day during that time doing the soul searching that is calling you now. It is time to get to know and rely on your inner wise self and make a commitment to change going forward.

Three sessions.

Three weeks.

Answer your call to change.

Week #1 - Embrace Yourself

This week, you will think about who you are and who you have become up until now. You will create a life's journey timeline depicting your experiences and what you have learned. You will answer a battery of targeted questions to allow you to really understand and recognize your own motivations, strengths, and attitudes and how they have been shaped.

Everything you have learned and experienced up until now has shaped who you are and who you have become. It has shaped your identity and who you consider yourself to be. Every interaction, every feeling, every thought, and every person you have encountered have been part of the story of *you*.

While this unique journey defines you and who you have become, it is not complete. The journey is constantly unfolding. When the thunderbolt strikes you and the ego mask identity you have come to equate with who you are is loosened, you begin to see the entirety of yourself more clearly. You become more aware of a deeper part of you that has always been with you and is an integral part of you are at your core. This wise self I have been referring to throughout these sessions has been

90

waiting for you to claim it and realize that it is a part of you that has been there before your life's journey started to unfold through your own experience of yourself. You are not only your experiences and what happens to you. You are a both product of your unique journey and you are also much bigger than that timeline of experience. Perhaps your experiences and everything you have learned up until now is designed to help you create the story of who you are destined to become and draw on all that knowledge you have gained to help you do that.

To do this, you must first reflect upon who you have become, embrace who you are now, and acknowledge everything you have learned that brought you here. In my work with leaders over the years, I frequently conducted a simple exercise with groups and teams to help them gain self-awareness and at the same time, see the deeper similarities amongst themselves and their seemingly different journeys. I would have everyone in the class take a flipchart piece of paper and a handful of markers and follow these instructions:

- Draw a timeline with pictures of your life's timeline on the page.

- Include where you grew up, key events that shaped you, key highlights, and any major defining moments that influenced who you are today.
- Do not make this just a resume or a job history; include all facets of yourself and your life.
- At the end of the timeline, answer these three questions on your flipchart page: What is most important to you? What next part of the story do you want to create? What holds you back?
- You will have 5-7 minutes to walk through your pictorial timeline and tell this story to us.

I have listened to literally thousands of leaders recount their journeys with this exercise. When I introduce it, I am often met by some with the usual reactive hesitancy, trepidation, or discomfort. "I can't draw." "What types of pictures do I need to draw?" "I can't do all this on one page." "I'm not sure how to do this."

I tell people to use their creativity and to remember that this is not an art competition, so not to worry about their perceived art skills. I always find it fascinating that the first thing most people worry about when faced with such an exercise is whether their artistic ability will measure up or not.

Less Ego, More Soul

In order to normalize the experience for everyone and to make it easier, I would show my own timeline and walk through my own story with everyone. The act of seeing someone else do it and be vulnerable and transparent actually helped people relax and go within to find and reflect on their own story and insights.

What I found from listening to thousands of these stories is that if we think about it, we all have different experiences in the progression of our life's journeys that have shaped our beliefs and realities, molded our ego mask identities, and influenced who we have become. We all have a story of who we are and how we arrived at where we are today. The uncanny thing was that in spite of all those different journeys that people shared, there was a deeper part of each one that everyone could resonate with. The things that people talked about as being most important to them were eerily the same for just about everyone. The yearning to contribute something more and make a bigger difference in the world was the same, despite their individual differences of socialization, culture, race, socioeconomic status, or gender. What held people back from becoming the next version of themselves they wanted to create was also similar.

Less Ego, More Soul

On a deeper level, despite the upbringings and economic statuses and achievements, almost everyone I encountered had noticeably common ground. Their wise selves, beyond the socialization, the varying paths, and the ego identity, spoke the same language.

In this first week of guided soul searching, get acquainted with what has made up your own journey up until now. Remember, we spend a good part of our lives shaping and strengthening our ego mask and learning to identify with it. While parts of our mask are actually our own, other parts of it have been shaped by what we have adapted ourselves to be. Another piece of it is simply an appearance that faces outward to the world and sends messages to others about who we are, whether we identify totally with that appearance or not.

Your goal from the Guided Soul Search Sessions is to examine and embrace the person you have become in the world, tap into the deeper inner wisdom you have access to, and to be more deliberate about integrating and creating the person you want to become. When I say this, it can sound much like the self-help mantra of "be the best you can be" you hear from the wide selection of self-improvement advocates. While that is, indeed, a worthy endeavor, that is not exactly what I am referring to here. I am not referring to just becoming your best version. I am referring to becoming your whole version. That is a very different proposition and endeavor.

By being whole, I mean:

- Awakening to the magnificence of your own existence
- Coming to terms with and embracing your individual journey and the legacy you have inherited from your unique upbringing and experiences
- Realizing that despite your uniqueness, you are not separate
- Understanding how you and other human beings are more the same than different
- Integrating the inner wisdom that connects you to everything
- Creating the self that you are called to be to allow you to contribute and serve fully

If that doesn't sound tangible or concrete enough, it may be because it isn't something you are used to considering or doing. This is more about who you are being rather than what you are doing. You may be so used to doing that you may not have given much thought to who you are being while you are doing all the things you are doing. What I am referring to here reverses the pattern. Who you are comes first. From that place, what you are doing takes on a whole different flavor.

To make this a bit more concrete, go ahead and take a stab at doing the journey timeline exercise I just outlined. Draw your own timeline on a large sheet of paper. You can do it on a blank piece of printer paper if you prefer and if that is easier. It doesn't matter what you draw it on. Don't let not having the right type of paper deter you from moving forward and doing this. I am displaying my own timeline here for an example so you can at least have an example to go by if you need it.

Some things to consider as you begin:

- Please do not focus on or compare artwork. The drawings can be simple stick figures or even shapes and symbols. They are there merely to provide a visual representation of key events in the chronology of your life, not to win an art contest.
- The timeline is not meant to include every key event or happening in your life either. It is meant to be a summary of events that brought you where you are today. This helps you see where you are, what shaped you, and think about where you want to head.

96

Here are the instructions once again.

My Journey Timeline Exercise

- Take a blank sheet of printer paper or a flipchart page.

- Gather a bunch of different colored markers to draw with.

- Draw a timeline with illustrations of your life's timeline on the page.

- Include in this timeline where you grew up, key events that shaped you, key highlights, and any major defining moments that influenced who you are today. It's your journey.

- Do not make this just a resume or a job history; include both personal and professional facets of yourself and your life.

- Be brief—this is a summary. No need to include everything in your life.

- As you draw the pictures, do a mental walk through of the timeline of events that brought you to where you are today.

- You can use different colored markers, one color, or just a black one.

- Be creative and use symbols or whatever representations come to your head

- At the end of the timeline — answer these three questions on your flipchart page: What is most important to you? What next part of the story do you want to create? What holds you back?

Example: Janet's Journey Timeline

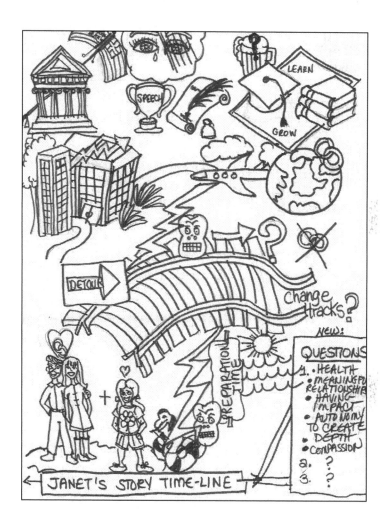

See the Story in the Journey

Once you've drawn the journey timeline, take a look at the events that you singled out and drew about as the events that brought you to where you are. Usually behind each event is a deeper story and shaping.

If you take a look at my journey timeline, for example, here's what is depicted in the pictures:

- ❖ I grew up in Athens, Greece in two worlds—with an American father and a Greek mother—both cultures and customs had a significant impact on my upbringing, beliefs, and socialization.
- ❖ An outward and temporary physical disability in elementary school caused me to go inward and become unusually self-reflective about human behavior and psychology at a young age.
- ❖ I went to an international high school with representation from twelve different countries—and learned to speak different langauges. This diversity socialized me to expect and appreciate difference.
- ❖ I loved school, loved writing and speaking and forensics—I competed in and won first place in several regional speech competitions with other schools. One of my award-winning speeches was a

motivational self-improvement type speech was entitled "Image, Society, and Man's Search for His Soul"—which is especially eerie as I consider this book I am writing right now.

❖ College was a difficult time for me as I went to the United States for the first time since the 6th grade. I had difficulty adapting to the teenage college culture—especially the culture of drinking. In Greece, there was no drinking age, so going out and getting drunk as the center of a party was not a focus. It seemed as if for my classmates drinking was the center of the social stage. After two years, I moved back to Greece and finished my degree at the University of Maryland overseas as a result— started working and moved right into getting a master's degree. Education and learning were always a big part of my life—I loved books and knowledge.

❖ While I was getting my master's degree, I met an Air Force officer in my classes. We got engaged six months later and were married when I was 23.

❖ I lived in Germany for several years and traveled throughout Europe while I lived there. I worked in a bank in various roles, including a loan officer while getting my second master's degree in business.

- ❖ When I came back to the United States, I worked in several large Fortune 200 companies in various leadership roles in organizational and leadership development and human resources—and kept pursuing my education in a PhD program in human development.
- ❖ The sudden illness and subsequent death of my father at age 62 was a major turning point in my life. It made me re-evaluate everything and derailed me for a while.
- ❖ I decided to end my marriage as a result of this re-evaluation. I quit the PhD program and was in dark time for over a year as a result of my dad's death. This period is a blur—like a derailment off a railroad track.
- ❖ I changed jobs and moved to yet another Fortune 200 company in a leadership and organizational development role. Here, I met my now husband, the love of my life. He was divorced with a 5-year old daughter, so I became a part-time step-mom. That was new for me, and yet another lesson in what I was teaching others over the years— influence without authority.
- ❖ Their divorce was less than amicable, so navigating the poison from my husband's ex-wife was an experience I was not prepared for and

taught me a whole new dimension of human behavior and taking the higher road.

❖ Another thunderbolt hit when my best friend's daughter, the same age as my step-daughter, died at the age of ten without warning. I was hit with the same type of force my father's death had produced. More re-evaluation. I realized that climbing the corporate ladder was not what I wanted to spend my life doing, even if the field I was in was the one I loved. I was a creator who needed autonomy and expression. So, I self-selected out of the leadership climb and began to prepare to create a business and brand more closely aligned with the impact I wanted to have on people and in the world.

❖ So here we are now. I am crystal clear about what is most important to me:

- Health—without our physical and mental health, we are unable to be or create anything.
- Meaningful relationships (this means deep, close relationships with people)
- Having impact
- Autonomy to create

- Depth (surface anything is not that appealing to me)
- Compassion (having empathy and understanding for others)

❖ The next part of the story I want to create is still unfolding. I think right now, I am living the story I wanted to create.

❖ At this point, the only things that hold me back are time and money, and frankly, trying to prioritize and operationalize the many creative ideas into things that are useful and tangible to others.

Now It's Your Turn

I provide this example for you so that now, you can do this exercise. Draw your journey timeline and then write out a summary in bullets of what you just depicted. This is a very brief depiction of how you got to this point in time and all the major events that brought you here. Of course, it doesn't include every detail, beautiful moment, trial and tribulation, but it is a summary. This is your journey. If you break up each component of your journey, there are specific learnings and things and people you encountered along the way that shaped who you have become.

Embracing Who You Have Become: Putting it All Together

You know that your journey up until now has shaped you into the person you are. Every choice you made, every experience you had, every mistake you made, every joy you heralded, and every person you encountered has contributed to who you have become. You have survived and you have thrived. You have laughed and suffered and risen and fallen. You have overcome and bounced back and created and prevailed. You have had dark days and bright ones, and through all of it, you have gained character, perspective and strength. You have also suffered wounds and scars and sometimes struggled to pull through. Regardless of what you have enjoyed and endured, all have brought you here. Here to the person you are. The person who you have become.

Part of growing and evolving is learning to let go of who we are now. How does a caterpillar become a butterfly? It is not by continuing along as a caterpillar. It goes into a cocoon and goes within—and an amazing metamorphosis occurs as a result. When it emerges from the cocoon, it is no longer a caterpillar. It is a butterfly. It retained some elements of its former self yet integrated itself into something new.

That is what you are being called to do with these Soul Search Sessions. To go deep within and find not just who you are, but also, who you are called to become. Then to do the deeper work that allows you to shed who you have become to move toward who you are *becoming*.

Before you can move on to integrating your whole self, you must be aware of and embrace what you have learned up until now. This is your journey. This timeline is a brief summary of that journey. So, as you look at your journey timeline up until now, reflect upon what you have learned and who you have become as a result of your unique path. As you look at what you wrote and drew, reflect and take this exercise deeper by answering the following questions. Include the good and not so good—don't filter these questions or candy-coat them, as the answers will help you later.

Childhood

1. How have my parents and my childhood shaped who I am today?

2. What lessons do I want to keep from them to this day?

3. What do I want to shed or let go of from that upbringing?

4. What early experiences have had a deep impact on me?

5. What did I learn from those experiences?

6. What do I want to carry forward?

7. What do I want to stop carrying?

Adolescence

1. What was I like as a teenager?

2. What was I really good at?

3. What did I like and dislike?

4. What came easily to me?

5. What was my biggest challenge during this period?

6. What did I learn during this period of my life?

7. What part of me from that time do I want to resurrect and bring forward?

8. What part of me from that time no longer serves me now?

Adulthood

1. How did I end up in my career?

2. What parts of my career journey am I most proud of?

3. What have I learned from my career experiences?

4. What am I most challenged by?

5. What have I learned from the relationships in my life?

6. What has given me the most joy?

7. What has caused me the most pain?

8. What have I learned about life?

9. What do I most need to let go of?

Now, take a look at the answers to the three questions you answered at the end of your journey timeline. What is most important to me? What next part of the story do I want to create? What holds me back? Spend some time looking at all that you wrote here.

Putting it All Together: Self-Reflection

1. What themes are emerging?

2. What are my greatest strengths?

3. What am I most proud of?

4. What parts of me do I want to nurture?

5. What is it time to let go of?

6. What words would I use to describe the person I have become?

As you look at the page, recognize yourself for all that you have experienced, learned, endured, contributed, and become. Recognize the light and the dark and the gray in between. Recognize yourself. And now, see yourself. *Fully.* You have come a long way! You are a survivor and a warrior and a powerhouse. You are not your parents, your upbringing, or your experiences. You are bigger. Much, much, bigger than any journey timeline or story can ever convey.

Embrace what brought you here and who you have become. Move towards who you are becoming. Answer the call to change.

Week #2 – Find Your Inner Wise Woman

This week will be the most uncomfortable because there isn't a tangible product to point to. This is the week you spend time tuning into the inner voice—the voice of the wise woman that is you. You will be provided numerous options of how to do this, including a powerful visualization tool and a host of probing questions. The bulk of this session consists of learning how to listen and practice introspection.

When I was in first grade, my teacher had all the students in the class draw a picture of what they wanted to be when they grew up. She then had each student stand up and show the drawing to the class and explain the vision's significance. I remember Jon's fireman with the bright red fire hat, Clara, the nurse, helping people heal in hospital beds, and even Laura's crown and robe as she explained her desire to be a queen. And while I have few memories of first grade, the picture I drew and what I said stands etched in my mind's eye as if it happened yesterday.

I wanted to be a "Magic Woman".

I remember the somewhat bewildered, amused, and interested look on my teacher's face as I explained what I deemed to be the female version of a magician: "I will have the power to heal people and help them be whatever they want with the touch of my wand."

When she heard my description, I remember her attempt to fit my description into a more conventional, rational sense, and say something like, "So, you want to be a doctor, someone who helps sick people get better?" To which I defiantly shook my head and answered, "No, not a doctor. I want to help people be whoever they want to be. Not just get over being sick." There was my vision, clear as day. A calling from the wise woman in the portal. Yet when I'd think back on that interaction, I'd laugh at the childish, silly description I had given of my calling.

What was a "Magic Woman" in the real world, really? Seriously. I, following my teacher's lead, dismissed it as fantasy. I gravitated toward the conventional, rational ways most of us do as we contemplate how to make a living and make our way in the world. I listened to the people around me whom I thought had the true answers. Of course, my teacher must have known what was best for me and what I was meant to be. She was a teacher! Teachers had the answers. Right?

It's funny, but over the years, every time I embarked on something that my vision of that "Magic Woman" would do, I felt joy. I felt I was contributing something valuable and serving something greater than myself. The Magic Woman would show up in my best work. Leading workshops on leadership or human development. Writing. Creating. Healing.

Every time I strayed from those activities and instead, engaged in climbing the corporate ladder and focusing on achieving title and status, I'd get beaten by my body. I could feel the beating as I would actually become physically ill and manifest some sort of physical illness. Difficulty breathing. Headaches. Stomach upsets. Neck pain.

"Listen to me," the voice in the portal inside of me was crying out to me.

"You are straying."

Even when I started my own business, which was something I supposedly did autonomously, I still didn't listen. Even then, I still had my magnificent ego identity mask to wear and my pleasing, polishing, and proving to do. I hired an expensive marketing strategist to convince me to do what everyone else was doing. To follow the conventional rules.

"Create an exclusive image so people think you are important. Change your website colors. Give people short lists of things because their attention spans are short. Grow your email list and blast people with your advertisements," I was told.

"Give people what they want. They want simple and quick."

It all made practical sense to the pleasing, polishing, and proving ego mask I was wearing. And it worked to gain followers and prestige and even fame. But it certainly wasn't what the Magic Woman would do. It was just like listening to my first-grade teacher all over again, telling me what I wanted to be was a doctor. My wise woman talking to me in the portal knew better. I didn't listen to her, though. I pushed the chair more tightly over the portal to block out her obviously clueless voice and proceeded with the seemingly more fitting advice given to me by those who helped me shape and perfect my successful ego identity. I marched along and thought things were going well for the most part. Until the thunderbolts hit.

Less Ego, More Soul

I talked about the death of my father, but there were two others, too. The sudden death of my best friend's daughter, at the age of ten. My own health scare that had me in the emergency room with a heart rate of 240 beats per minute.

When these thunderbolts struck, I was electrocuted. As I mentioned earlier, I had to stop in my tracks and listen. My ego mask identity was not in alignment with my wise self. There was a big disconnect. The things I did to succeed and thrive on the outside was not what I needed to succeed and thrive as a whole. I had convinced myself that they were. My wise self knew better. I just had to learn to access her and listen—and integrate her voice into my ego identity. I had to learn to trust her and seek her counsel.

This is no easy feat for achievers. Sitting and just being means complacency. It means time wasting. We think it takes away from our incredibleness. Our incredible competence at pleasing, polishing, and proving just how incredible we are at doing.

Learning to listen to our deeper, wise self is hard work because we are trained to listen to our programmed minds for what is relevant to a preconceived desired outcome that we are so good at setting. We are listening

116

for answers that will help us achieve our goals and lead us to a successful outcome that will maintain our sense of control. This new type of listening I am referring to here requires a detachment from outcomes. It has no clear-cut goal product.

It is a surrender.

Yikes! How? Tuning into your senses and the natural world is a good place to start. Learning to listen means finding the spot in yourself that accesses the portal to the ancient wise person that already lives within you. It is always accessible and is not part of the ego mask you have created as your identity.

When you read books on mindfulness or meditation, those practices are not there just as a tool to relieve anxiety or stress. They are tools to help you go beyond the thoughts and noise in your own mind and transcend your own ego identity. The practices ultimately help you learn to listen. The key in learning to listen is that there is not one way to tap into this place of inner wisdom. What you are ultimately trying to do when you do this is to filter out stories you have been taught or you have created about what is important.

This does not need to be as a result of a thunderbolt experience. This wise self that resides within you is always there, and you can access it at any time. You just need to learn how.

Integrating your senses, writing and visualization, the following section provides you a few select options of how to tap into and listen to this voice.

You can pick one or all of these activities during this week's session, as the point is not to just participate in a bunch of activities. The point is to put yourself into a contemplative and meditative state where you are still, and quiet your conscious mind so that you can find and listen to your inner voice.

Option #1: Tap in through Your Senses

You habitually rely on your mind to guide you. The problem is that your mind has been programmed by the same program you used to build your ego mask identity. In order to access the original operating system that connects you to your deeper wisdom, you must usurp and even turn off that ego programming. Fortunately, your own senses are already keenly attuned to this inner portal of wisdom and know how to do that. They are ready-made, detour pathways you can use to tap into the inner portal of wisdom and listen.

Your senses consist of not only sight, hearing, taste, touch and smell—but also of your sixth sense of intuition. Intuition is tricky because we often think our conscious mind and the programming and fears we have is our voice of intuition. Intuition is not that programmed voice of caution that results from a prior emotional experience ingrained in your mind. When you are afraid to fly on a plane because you have a feeling that something bad will happen, for example, that is not intuition. That is usually a programmed fear acting out in your brain, resulting from some emotional experience your conscious mind had recorded and wired. Intuition is much deeper than your one unique experience like that.

119

Intuition is a part of your mind that goes beyond your conscious awareness or experience into a collective unconscious that houses programming that is unique to all human beings. It is a deeper knowing that comes from somewhere you can't even explain. Think of something you just know instinctively but aren't sure how you know it. Mothering, for example. While we now have an array of books on how to be a mother ("what to expect when we are expecting", and the like), there is an intuitive knowing in every psychologically healthy woman who becomes a mother. She doesn't need a guidebook to tell her what to do; she just knows. Sixth sense. You must learn to tap into and listen to all six of your senses.

Before you begin, buy a small notebook and clip a pen to it. A notebook small enough to put into your pocket is best, or if you are a woman carrying a purse, something you can easily slip into your purse without weighing it down. Don't use the notes application on your smartphone to take notes for this, however. Once you pull out your phone, you may be distracted by an email, a text, a news notification, or other social media applications you are addicted to monitoring throughout the day. Carry this notebook with you everywhere. Use it to record what is coming up for you during each of the following activities. Don't overthink what to write and don't edit your entries. Just record what you are thinking, feeling, and/or experiencing as you participate.

Take a Walk in Nature
Whether it is a hike in the woods amongst trees, a stroll along the beach, a walk alongside a mountain or canyon, or a roam around a park, nature speaks the language of our inner portal. There is research study after research study that demonstrates the healing power of nature on human beings.

Take a 30-minute walk and stare at the ocean, feel the breeze on your skin, watch the birds soaring over your head, or bask in the shade of the trees towering over your head. Look at the array of colors in the flower beds you pass, blooming like a natural art show. Take deep breaths and smell the scents that you would never take notice of. As you do this, your raw senses take over your mind, and your connection to a universal energy deepens. You can feel the aliveness in everything around you, and recognize your deeper connection to it all, without really understanding how. *You just know.* That's the place you are looking for.

Some of you reading this may be thinking that this sounds a bit too new age-y or ethereal. If you are thinking that, you are operating from your judging ego identity. Listen more deeply without your mind jumping to judge what you are experiencing. Just look, smell, hear, and feel the beauty around you and allow yourself to connect to this beauty. This is the path to the portal of wisdom.

Allow your mind to be still while you just look around with awe at everything you see.

Notice: What feelings are coming up for you? What is becoming clear to you?

After 30 minutes, find a place to sit down and pull out your notebook. Write down your answers to those questions. Write down anything else you are noticing. Write down what you are thinking. Just write. Unfiltered, without judgment. Listen to what is coming up and write it down. The key is not to think too hard, but just to write. For how long? For however long it takes, but if you need a boundary, write for no less than ten minutes.

A few more ideas for practices that will tap into your senses are listening to soft music, meditating and gardening. Whatever it is that you practice, be fully present when you are engaging in it. Don't look at your smartphone or distract yourself with a to-do list. This is your time to be fully aware of your senses and to tap into a part of yourself that you may have neglected as a pathway. You are getting to know a deeper, wiser part of yourself that may seem foreign yet familiar. This part of yourself does not speak the language you are conditioned with. Part of learning to listen is to realize that you may need to translate the meaning of what you are hearing— and that can take time. Practice your writing exercise for ten minutes right after your practice and record what you hear. Again, don't worry if it doesn't make sense or there isn't anything your ego identity doesn't find to be profound. Later, you will take all the things you wrote and use them to answer your own questions. *Later.*

Option #2: Tap in through Writing

Your unconscious mind has a direct line to your inner wisdom, and its messages are often transmitted through symbols and creative expressions.

How often do you spend time to tune into these messages that are sent through creative channels? Do you even know how to do that?

When you do tap into this creative frequency, you may find information that is surprisingly relevant to the questions you are wrestling with. A pathway to learn to listen to your inner wisdom is to tap into the symbolic messages and innate creativity that is constantly bubbling in your unconscious mind.

Journal Writing Exercise

One of the easiest ways to tap into the frequency of your inner wisdom through this unconscious creative channel is through writing. Writing down what comes to you without much thought or effort is a way of channeling your internal voice and translating it into words to be able to examine it externally.

I remember receiving my first journal as a gift at the age of ten. It was a 6 X 9 hardbound pink book with blank white pages and fastened in the front with a mini

124

lock and key. "My Diary" was written in bold gold leaf letters across the front of it. I was so excited to get it since I loved to write poetry and short stories. It was a book of my own that I could create from scratch. Yet, as I sat with the newfound blank book in my room, the excitement turned to anxiety at my first attempt to write in it.

What are you supposed to write in a diary, I remember wondering.

I had this beautiful blank book ready for me to create whatever I wanted with. This diary was for me only. I was never of shortage for creative ideas, stories, and imagination. I made up characters constantly and had a whole cast of characters living in my head. When faced with an object designed specifically to record it all in, however, my reaction was that I wanted to make sure that I used it correctly. I was looking for the "right" way to keep a diary. Was I supposed to record what I did each day? Could I just write down my thoughts, or was it supposed to be a recording of my activities? Wanting to know the rules to be sure I was "good" was evident even in my attempts to execute my creative expression.

I summoned the images in my head from television characters who had diaries in their storylines as models for what a diary was and should contain. I recalled that these characters would start by writing the date at the top of the page, and begin their entries with the words, "Dear Diary". Then they would record on the page what they did that day. As a ten-year old, I assumed I had discovered the "right" way to keep a diary and I dutifully followed that template. Since this method didn't really resonate with my own creative self-expression, I did that for a few months, became bored of it, and abandoned the diary altogether. It joined the other first coveted and then discarded items brimming in my childhood closet. I definitely wasn't accessing my own deeper wisdom and creative expression with the forced diary exercise. I was stuck in the pleasing and proving parts of the ego identity I was in the midst of forming.

Years later, as an adolescent, what is often referred to as journal writing awakened for me in a more resonate way. I think I read somewhere at the time that many of the poets and writers I so admired all had kept journals to record their thoughts, ideas, and the like. They used these journals as unstructured vehicles to unleash their emotions and thoughts and to allow their creative process to emerge. As a result, I decided to start seriously using writing as a way to provide a space for my own creative instincts to emerge. I bought a blank book with lined pages and began to record whatever was coming up for me. My only rule was to write in it every day—regardless of whether I felt like it or not—as to maintain consistency. I wrote about what I was feeling. I wrote poetry and prose. I wrote down quotes or passages that struck me or that spoke to me in a deep way. I wrote down observations. I wrote down questions that I had or things that I was observing about my environment, my surroundings, myself, and about life in general. It was an attempt to record and put on paper the daily workings of my inner world.

I still have all of the journals I have written over the years since then. When I read through the pages at what I wrote in those formative years, there are amazing glimpses of the deeper wisdom that already resided inside. Even as an adolescent with much more experiencing and growing up to do, I could see glimmers of an inner source of knowing well beyond my years bubbling up in my words.

The point of keeping some sort of writing journal is to actually put to paper what is going on inside of you—to help make the deeply internal come to light and put on paper for examination and translation. There is really no template or right way to do this. In light of the commonalities I observed in thunderbolt experiences, however, there are key questions that may be begging for you to explore further.

Here is one way to do that:

- Designate a blank or lined notebook as your soul searching recorder journal. You can use the same notebook you use for the other exercises in this book as to keep all your notes together. Or you can keep this one separate. Do whatever works best for you.

- Take the 13 questions listed below and write each one on a separate blank page in the book. Give yourself about four blank pages between each question.

- Spend dedicated quiet time with these questions and write what is coming up for you as you ask these questions of yourself. Don't overthink them.

- Don't rush through this. Sit still and get quiet. Really reflect inward. Don't try to impress yourself with your own answers. This is not a competition and there is nothing to win with a "right" answer. You are moving past the right and wrong and the winning and competing here. You are searching into your soul. Your wisest self is waiting to talk with you!

- You don't have to answer all the questions at once. Perhaps you want to think about one question a day and write what comes up for you daily. The key is to be consistent and not to let too much time go by. Strike while the iron is hot, and the portal is open from your thunderbolt experience.
- Use the rest of the pages to record anything else that comes up for you each day—whether it is a thought, an observation, a quote, a poem, or something that moves you. Whatever it is, write it down. You are attempting to record the inner stirrings that are happening and capture the whispers you hear trying to communicate with you.

Here are the 13 questions to journal about:

1. What am I feeling?

2. What am I thinking?

3. What is feeling important now?

4. What is feeling unimportant now?

5. What am I learning about myself?

6. What prescribed stories do I carry about what is real and true?

7. What seems real and true to me now?

8. What do I truly value?

9. What do my daily actions tell me and others about what I value?

10. What do I want to change about myself?

11. What do I want to change in my actions?

12. How can I live more in alignment with what is important?

13. What must I do differently now?

Option #3: Tap in through Visualization

Another powerful way to tap into your unconscious creative and receive messages from your inner portal of wisdom is to practice visualization. You might have heard stories or even experienced firsthand how impactful visualization can be. Athletes do it to up their games and play at their best. Singers do it to get over stage fright and kill it on stage. Numerous studies show that visualizing yourself practicing something can lead to results similar to actually practicing it.

Using a specific visualization exercise as a direct way to access the portal to your inner wise self is taking the practice a step deeper. Because of the nature of the work I have chosen, I have been introduced to and practiced many visualization exercises over the years. Many of them are designed to help you tap into your inner wise self, and actually picture the voice inside of you as an actual person. When I participated in formal coaches training at the Coaches Training Institute years ago, I was re-introduced to a type of visualization exercise that proved to be an incredibly powerful tool to tap into the wise woman residing inside of me. This visualization exercise tapped into the inner voice from the portal that I have been referring to and gave me a pathway to access the portal more easily and readily. This is especially

132

valuable during this Guided Soul Search Session, as you are learning to access, listen to, and trust your inner wisdom during these three weeks.

I can still, to this day, see the wise version of myself who spoke to me during the visualization exercise I did in the class, and as a result, have a tool to use to access her more readily and often. She was the "Magic Woman", the one I had known so well back in my elementary school aged attempts to describe who I wanted to be when I grew up. She was there all along. I finally got to meet her during this visualization exercise.

The exercise was designed to help you access your future self—conceptually letting you meet yourself ten years in the future. While the visualization takes you to a point twenty years in the future, it actually allows you to talk to your wiser self, right now. It taps into a part of yourself that already knows what you value, what is important and not important, and who you are being called to be. The future aspect of it is there to help you separate your current ego identity self and look at your wiser self in some future state. It is not fortune-telling or predicting the future, as some people may try to view it as. It is an exercise to help you access and talk to the part of yourself that is beyond your ego identity—the person you are meant to become who is already there, guiding you along, if you learn to listen and interpret.

You may be a bit skeptical as you hear this, as your logical, rational mind may have trouble with the squishiness of how this sounds. It may sound new age-y or something that hippy or bohemian types do, not something that serious, logical people engage in. The discomfort makes sense, since most of us are not used to accessing our own unconscious minds and understanding its language of symbols. The language it speaks is jumbled and isn't directive or definitive, so it can feel muddled and confusing. It is like trying to interpret a code we don't understand, or even a foreign language we don't have the comprehension of. Don't let the discomfort and unfamiliarity discourage you. Just relax your mind and go with it. Remember, all of these exercises may be out of your comfort zone. Don't expect to be comfortable. Expect to listen, learn, grow, and change.

I have adapted and created slightly different versions of this exercise with clients over the years, and what I find is that it usually delivers an incredibly impactful and almost uncanny experience for those that do it. You can do it on your own with the same effect; you don't need someone else to guide you through it. To make it more impactful, I suggest that you audio-tape yourself reading the instructions, and then play it for yourself while you close your eyes and follow your own instructions.

Here is one of the visualization exercises I use, adapted from the Future Self exercise for coaches that I learned from Coach Training Institute, I have changed it a bit from the original one found in the coaches materials provided during the coach training program.

Visualization Exercise to Access Future Self

Get into a comfortable position. Now, allow your eyes to close and begin to focus your awareness on your breath. Breathe in and breathe out. Each breath allows you to become more relaxed. As you sink deeper down into quiet and ease, perhaps you can imagine a cable, a cord running down from the back of your spine. Imagine it going down to the center of the earth. Deep into the earth. Imagine there is something that you can anchor the cable to, so that no matter where you go on your inner journey, you feel solidly connected to the earth.

As you allow yourself to go deeper into a state of relaxation, remember a time when you stood before a pond or a lake and it was quiet and peaceful. You may have dropped a pebble into the center and noticed the ripples rippling out. One ripple after another, flowing outward farther and farther. The ripples slowing down, becoming further apart until the water once again is calm and peaceful.

Imagine that your body is like that body of water and as you drop a pebble into the center of your body, you can feel ripples of relaxation, waves of relaxation flowing through your body, up through your torso into your chest and your back. Up through the vertebrae and spreading out into each and every muscle of your back. Through your shoulders and arms, up through your neck, your jaw, and your face. Feeling those ripples relax you as your muscles let go and become soft and loose. Feel the ripples of relaxation flowing down through your abdomen, your pelvis, down through your thighs, your calves, your ankles and your toes. As you become more relaxed, you are quiet and peaceful.

Now, bring your attention to a spot between your eyes, a third eye. Imagine a light there. What color is the light between your eyes? Now, perhaps you can imagine that light becoming a beam that extends out into space. Follow that beam as it leaves where you are sitting and as it travels out into the city. Follow that beam as it continues out so you can see the land, the mountains and then the coastline. Keep on going further and further out into space and notice the curvature of the Earth. As you keep going further and further out, find yourself enveloped by the softness and quiet of space. Notice below you the blue green earth with white clouds in wisps all around it.

Allow yourself to enjoy this gentle perspective for a moment.

Now, notice another beam of light very near to you, one with a different color from the one that took you out into space. Begin to follow this new beam back down to earth. This beam is taking you back to earth ten years from now. It is going ten years into the future. Keep following this beam down. Notice the curvature of the earth the wisps of cloud—the oceans and lands stretched out below you.

As you come closer to the end of this beam of light, notice where you are. This is where your most positive Future Self lives. This is you, ten years from now. As you come down further, notice the land around you. Notice where you are. Notice what nature surrounds you. Notice what dwelling is near. Now move to the dwelling of your Future Self. What does it look like? What kind of landscape is there? Are there trees? Flowers? What kind? Get a sense of this place.

Now, walk to the dwelling and do what you need to do to get someone to come to the door. Know that on the other side of the door is your Future Self waiting to greet you. It is you, ten years from now. As the door opens, what do see? What do you notice? Greet your Future Self and notice the way your Future Self returns your Greeting. Notice how you are welcomed into this time and place ten years in the future. Take in this person. This is your future self. Move with your Future Self to a comfortable place for a visit. Perhaps your Future Self offers you something to drink. Settle in and make yourself comfortable for a conversation with your Future Self. There are some questions you might want to ask. Begin by asking—What is it, Future Self, that you most remember about the last ten years? Listen to the answer. Ask: What stands out most in your memory? Take a moment and listen to the answer. Ask your Future Self another question: What do I need to get from where I am now, to where you are?

Listen to the answer. Now ask: What is most helpful for me to know in order to get to where you are? Listen as your Future Self talks to you. Now take a moment and ask your Future Self your own questions. What else would you like to ask?

Now, ask your Future Self one final question before you go: What name, other than your first name, are you called by? Do you have a special name, a symbol, a word, or a phrase? What is this name? Now bring this visit with your Future Self to a close. Thank them for being here with you today. Thank them for the wisdom and say goodbye.

Now, find your way back to the beam of light that brought you here. Journey back up this beam, watching this world ten years in the future grow smaller and ever smaller as you move out into space. Marvel again, at the blue green of the earth below you and the clouds swirling.

Now, notice a new beam of light, a new beam that will take you back to the present time—back to where you started. Follow this beam of light back to the present time on this Earth. As you travel down this beam, notice the earth growing bigger and bigger. Notice the lands and oceans. Notice the skyline of where you currently live, and finally, you are back in this room you are sitting in.

Now, get ready to count from 3 to 1. Once you reach the count of 1, you can open your eyes and will be refreshed and alert, as if you have had the perfect amount of rest, knowing you can remember everything you wish of this journey. When you open your eyes, try to be silent for a moment and then jot down everything you remember about your journey.

Start the count.

Three, coming back to present time, becoming more alert and refreshed.

Two, stretching out, stretching your body and feeling the ground beneath you.

One, open your eyes.

Be silent for a moment. Take your journal notebook and write down everything you remember. Specifically, see if you can remember the answer to these questions:

1. What did your Future Self look like? Act like?

2. Where did they live?

3. What did the house look like?

4. What answers did they give you to the questions you asked?

5. What did you feel like talking to them?

6. What was the name or symbol for you them shared with you?

Put It All Together

From the three practices in this session, you have
spent time recording your thoughts, reactions, feelings,
and insights. At this point you should have sufficient
material to self-reflect on the messages you have
gathered from your inner wise self.

Take your notebook, sit in a place where you are
comfortable and won't be disturbed. You can go outside
if that puts you in a more relaxed mood. Take a few deep
breaths and look over all the notes you have taken over
the course of this week from the exercises you
participated in. You may not have done all the
exercises—that doesn't really matter. Take what you
have and read through them. Pay attention to the words
you used and the tone and the themes of what you wrote
down. Notice the feeling you get when you read over it
all. Don't allow your mind to criticize or judge what you
wrote—stay away from your tendency to want to jump to
evaluation. You are not evaluating here. You are
processing. There is a difference between evaluating and
processing. Processing is allowing yourself to take in all
the information in front of you without filtering it.

Now that you've had a chance to read through all your notes, open your notebook and write down your answers to the following questions:

1. What themes come up for me from the learning to listen exercise?

2. What am I realizing is most important to me?

3. How would I act differently if I focused on what is most important?

4. What have I focused on now that is relatively unimportant in the larger scheme of things?

5. What drives the disconnect from what is most important in my day-to-day actions?

6. What do I want to embrace more fully?

7. What has shaped who I am and how I behave up until now?

8. Which current beliefs, behaviors, and habits do I currently hold and exhibit that are not aligned with my inner wise self?

9. What words of wisdom do I need to internalize and live by?

10. What gifts am I called to contribute to the world?

11. What is the name I would give my wise self?

12. Who am I becoming now?

13. What old stories do I need to let go of to move more fully towards who I am becoming?

The answers to these questions are your result from your second week of Guided Soul Search Sessions. Sit with them. Go inside yourself and really feel the answers. Find that place of inner knowing and let your pen do the rest. Trust that you already know the answers to these questions. *You do.*

Now, hold fast to these answers. You are ready to define who you are becoming beyond the ego mask in the last week of your guided soul searching.

Week #3 - Create Your Personal Manifesto

If you have spent the self-reflection time and have participated fully in these Guided Soul Search Sessions so far, the past couple of weeks have been intense. It can be difficult and even painful to go deep and do this type of self-introspection. You are seriously putting your life and who you are under a glaring light and probing microscope. Chances are you have rarely done this type of inner questioning and evaluation. While it may be uncomfortable and disorienting, it is also liberating and freeing at some level. You are in a process of discovery and at the brink of what can be a major turning point in your life. You have been shaken and are being called to change.

You have spent much of your life learning how to make your way in the world. You have accumulated stories others have given you and have carefully filtered them and incorporated parts of them into the ego identity you have created for yourself. These stories include your beliefs, your assumptions, your definitions of success, and your opinions about just about everything. Now is the time to re-evaluate all of these things that you had held to be true or had just adapted as "normal" or what you "should" do. You have spent time reflecting upon who you have become over all these years—what has shaped you and what you have learned. You have spent time uncovering the voice of your inner wise self that has been dormant or hidden most of the time and learning to access the wisdom that lies there. As a result of this questioning, you should now begin to see patterns in the answers you are discovering.

Everything you have experienced and learned up until now brings you to this point. It is finally time to befriend your inner wise self and put them in the front seat with you. Your ego identity is still the driver, but your inner wise self will be the navigator. You are headed in the same direction, together. You are ready to stop shutting them out, but instead, to make them a full partner in the rest of your journey. You are ready to co-create the rest of the path together—fully integrated as one voice.

This means re-establishing yourself to include your wise self in who you are being called to become. It means intentionally choosing who you want to be going forward and creating and continuously molding for yourself the compass you will follow. It means taking full accountability for your actions and striving to have your choices each and every moment be in alignment with this new identity that you are becoming. It means answering the call to be much bigger than the small dramas you allow yourself to play in and see the larger impact each one of your actions has around you—and in the world. You are not just who you have become up until now. Who you are becoming is much bigger and is not limited by your individual experiences. You have so much more to learn, create, and contribute and are part of something much larger than the interactions or things you have learned so far. You are limitless. Your wise self is the doorway to tapping into those expansive possibilities.

All of this may sound humongous. It may sound unrealistic or unproven. It's just not tangible enough. You may have had many "aha" moments from your exercises and the soul search questions in the sessions you just participated in but are having trouble operationalizing it all into your day-to-day life. You are still pushing to box yourself into something smaller, less ambiguous, and more comfortable. Something more familiar and more known and conventional.

"What do I do next?" is a likely question that you are struggling with.

This makes sense, as our conscious minds have trouble containing and holding the infinite potential that lies within each of us. I'm not sure any of us will ever be able to fathom just how big we are. For centuries, man has been grappling with the vastness of our existence and making up stories to survive and feel more comfortable with the unknown elements we still, to this day, can't explain. All we can do is try to expand our own lenses and at least listen to and integrate that part of ourselves that is so much bigger than our ego self. We can learn to behave and live more in trust and alignment with that part of ourselves. We still have to live in the real world and function on a day-to-day basis in society. We must adapt and influence and survive in the reality that exists in the material and conventional world. But how we choose to show up in this world and the presence we choose to embrace and embody is of our own making.

The rejection of what we have learned from others and hold as true up until now is the hardest first part of answering this call to change. Moving beyond conventional thinking about what is most important, who we are, and who we should be is a difficult task in moving towards really integrating your wise self and continuing to grow.

Plato, a well-known ancient Greek philosopher born in 427 BC, a famous student of Socrates, and one of the most important influencers of Western thought, explains this challenge we face in his classic writing known as the "Allegory of the Cave". Here is a brief summary of this poignant example of the challenge we all face when we move away from conventional thinking and learn to see the world differently than the way we were taught or socialized with.

Imagine three prisoners sitting chained inside a cave with their backs against a low wall, unable to move. They are sitting with a tall cave wall right in front of them. They cannot see behind them because of the way and position in which they are chained, but a big fire burns on a platform beyond the much lower wall behind them. This fire casts shadows on the wall in front of them. Behind the low wall behind them, there is a road, and there are various puppeteers who hold up books, objects, and puppets to entertain the public passing on the road where the wall is. The prisoners cannot see or even hear the puppeteers. Thus, they do not see the books, objects, or puppets. All they see are shadows of all these things flickering on the wall in front of them being reflected by the fire. They do not really know what these shadows are, but think they do. They make up a meaning of each of the objects and may even call them by a name. They are convinced that these shadows are real and that they know what they are. They recognize them and they are familiar, so they expect to see them.

One of the prisoners is freed and gets up and turns around. He sees the fire and the low wall and is disoriented. What could that possibly be? He then walks up and over the low wall to the street, where he sees the sun, the fire, and the puppeteers with all the objects. What he thought to be true was totally different now that he had a bigger perspective of the whole picture.

He rushes in to tell the other prisoners the truth about what they were seeing, and they become angered and fearful, believing he has gone mad and is dangerous. They have not seen what he has seen and are comfortable with the reality of the story they have made up about the meaning of the shadows. This new story does not fit with the reality they have believed day after day, year after year, so they immediately reject it as false. Even if this new reality is liberating, it is still hard to fathom. They even refuse to free themselves, as they are content with the explanations they have created to explain their environment and experience.

Misalignment Realization

This story is a perfect depiction of what the majority of us do to some degree. The question that arises for you now is which of the stories you are living by are no longer or were never in alignment with who you are becoming? Which stories are you ready to reject and move away from, now that you have seen past the shadows reflected on the wall?

Let me give you an example from my own life. As I reflected on this allegory of the cave and asked myself the same questions, I recalled this instance where I had a misalignment realization. It had struck me hard at the time, and I felt the harsh gap between what I believed to be important, what I was being taught, and what was actually being practiced around me.

As I mentioned, I grew up in Athens, Greece. I was socialized in two main cultures, both the Greek culture coming from my mother and the country we resided in, and the American culture from my dad's upbringing. I attended an English-speaking International school, so a bunch of other cultures were thrown into the mix. The Greek culture took a front seat for me due to fact that we lived in the country, I was baptized into the Greek Orthodox Christian faith, and so many of my mother's friends and relatives were of course Greek. It was weird though, because most of the Greeks didn't think I looked Greek and thought I had a foreign accent when I spoke

Greek, even if I did so fluently. As a result, they saw me as *xeni*, or foreign. The double bind was that the kids at school who were from the United States didn't see me as American since my mother was Greek, so they saw me as foreign, too. There was a special bond between all of us kids who were "Greek-American" living in Greece, as we lived and learned in two worlds, and we understood the outsider feeling that left you with in either culture. We used words from both languages when we spoke to each other to best express ourselves. We understood what it meant to blend norms from both cultures and tried our best to integrate what seemed like opposite customs or beliefs in some cases. To do this, we looked for similarity, not for difference. We saw the commonality in the religious customs, in the family norms, and just about everything. We tried not to see one way as right or the other wrong, but as two different ways or stories about the same thing. And yet, this made us different. It made us the one that stood out from each community we were trying to fit into. Contrasting ways of doing things had its advantage as well, as you could more easily see the story from afar since you were simultaneously being socialized in two worlds. I think this may have made me question things more readily at an early age.

Less Ego, More Soul

I remember an instance when I was fourteen years old and it was August 15, a holy day in Greece, and is celebrated as a national and religious holiday in the Greek Orthodox Christian tradition that honors Mary, the mother of Jesus. Across the country people flock to churches that bear her name to light a candle in her honor and kneel in front of an icon with her image. Many believe this holy day is a day of healing and praying to Mary can bear miracles.

My mother drove me and my sister, who was about six years old at the time, to a church on the top of a high hill in Athens to pay homage and respects to Mary on this holy day. As we approached the church, there was a long line of about fifty people long waiting to get inside the door. I remember hearing people complaining about the line and quite a few people pushing to cut in front of others. I kept distracted playing word games with my sister as we waited over an hour to enter the doorway. It was a beautiful yet simply constructed church, built of white marble with a terracotta roofed dome and a grand cross at the top. As we approached the door, a loud commotion ensued. Several middle-aged women standing ahead of me in line started pushing each other, each insisting she was ahead of the other in line. They started yelling insults and one even began using profanity as she admonished the other. All the while, I could see others rushing in front of them to kneel at and kiss the gilded icon that bore Mary's image. One woman pushed the other so hard she fell, and the one who had pushed her ran to take her place in front of the icon. I remember feeling horrified at the sight of this spectacle.

I turned to my mother and said, "I'm leaving, this is crazy."

My mother was furious at me to put it mildly, as we had waited for over an hour to get to the entrance, but I was unusually defiant. She stayed put with my sister as I made my way out of the entrance and walked back down the steep hill the church stood on to wait in front of the car until they finished paying homage.

In that moment, I was struck with a haunting misalignment between the obedient good girl and my wise inner self. My wise woman was telling me that there was something terribly off here. I was learning the virtues of kindness and loving thy fellow man and neighbor from the teachings of the church, which I believed to be true—yet the behaviors I was seeing modeled from those around me who were espousing those virtues were not in alignment. The walk did not follow the talk.

Less Ego, More Soul

Those ladies in the church might seem like an extreme case and not the norm, but I highlight the experience to make a point. We all may fall into this trap over time—we behave reactively and out of alignment with what we say we truly value. Our actions don't always match what we think or say is important. And often, what we think or say is important isn't what we truly believe or isn't consistent with the deep inner compass—the wise self beyond our external ego identity.

In that example, I can be dismissed as a righteous teenager without much life experience judging with absolute terms an isolated situation that was unfortunate to witness. Perhaps that was the case. Regardless, the reaction I had that day was the voice of my wise self coming forward to guide alignment. It was detecting a disconnect between the action I was about to take and the belief the action was serving—and it was calling it out for me to see.

Over the years, we learn to rationalize our actions and dismiss and ignore this voice when we are behaving out of alignment with what we say is most important. And as I mentioned, sometimes we aren't even tuned into what we believe is truly important, what beliefs are our own, and who we want to be.

Less Ego, More Soul

Thinking of that example made me realize that I did hear that wise woman inside of me much more often than I realized. She had called me and others out on the discrepancies of my actions over the years. I had to take a firmer stand and not just hide her but integrate her more fully to guide me.

Through this wake-up call of sorts, or what I call thunderbolt event, you have set aside your ego identity and been called to look deeper to sort this misalignment out. The exercises, self-reflection and practices you have spent the past two weeks wrestling with are bringing you closer to bridging the gap of this misalignment you have come to view as normal. They have brought you out of your comfort zone and habitual life and forced you to question everything. The result of this is to define for yourself what truly is important, what living and acting in alignment really looks like, and how you will hold yourself accountable to this inner compass you have now created.

It is time to create your own compass informed by the integration of all that you have experienced and learned up until now, the voice of your inner wise self, who you are, and what you are here to contribute. In this final Soul Search Session, it is time to take everything you have reflected upon and create your own personal manifesto to live by.

This is probably the point where we likely get into semantics and the desire to do things the "right way" again. What exactly is a manifesto? What is it supposed to look like? What must it include?

Simply put, and in this context right here, a manifesto is a declaration of your intentions and beliefs, and a guide to what is most important. It provides you with a reminder of what you say is important, and the actions that you will commit to take that are in alignment with that.

When you create this manifesto, you are creating an accountability check for yourself. Are you integrating your inner wisdom and the soul-searching questioning you have done into your everyday choices? Do your words, actions, and how you interact with others match what you say is important? It is a decision-making guide above everything else. It reminds you of your intentions and what course of action to take when you are at a choice point.

Why do this and how does this relate to everything we have been talking about so far?

Over the course of Week #1 and Week #2, you have done some deeper self-reflection and spent time evaluating who you are. They have helped you tap into and excavate your inner wise self and listen to the messages they bring you to who you are becoming. The manifesto you will create now seeks to operationalize answers to the questions into a personal code for the person you are becoming will live by. This manifesto integrates your wise self into the decisions you will make going forward, so that you draw on the whole, wise self that you are to serve as your life's compass.

This is an incredibly powerful exercise, as I have each person stand up and declare to the rest of the participants what they wrote. Some people break down in tears when they read it aloud, it is such an emotional experience.

Are you ready for ultimate alignment in your life? Now, it is time to make your self-reflection concrete in the form of your personal manifesto. You can add more if you like, but for the purposes of adding some structure and a tangible example, I provide you with this model. You can make it as long or as short as you like. The feedback I have received from those doing this exercise is that they like the notion of having it all fit on one page, as it makes it easier to refer to and even display. But this is your document, so feel free to ditch the model and create your own template. For those of you who find the template useful as a guide to follow, I will also offer the personal manifesto I created as a real example of what it potentially looks like when completed.

Sample Framework for your
PERSONAL MANIFESTO

My Personal Manifesto (You can put your actual name instead of the word "My" if it makes it more real and personal for you.)

Who I Am

In this section, write out statements that describe who you are at the core. What is your superpower, and what are you meant to contribute to the world? Use metaphors if you like, and don't be humble or shy. Integrate the full power of your inner wise self and combine it with your ego identity and all the things that have prepared you to embody this energy. Define who you really are at the deepest core.

What I Believe

In this section, write what you believe in. Not what others told you to believe, not what you think you should believe, but what your deepest, wisest self tells you are your universal beliefs. What are the things that transcend your culture, your socialization, and your personal preference that you want to see embodied in the world? Be bold here—write from notes you have taken over the past two sessions.

What I Am Committed To

What are you committed to? Who are you committed to being? What ideals are you committed to? What behaviors are you committed to trying to model?

As you write all of this down, be bold and don't play small. Don't keep yourself small. Think about the visualization exercise you did where you came face-to-face with your wise self embodied and integrated with your ego self. Bring that forward as you write. This is not the time to be worried about what others think or what you may sound like. Let yourself emerge and shine forth on the page.

Here's the manifesto I created when I did this soul search session exercise myself.

Janet's PERSONAL MANIFESTO

Who I Am

I am a modern-day alchemist here to help people transform their lives to gold. I am a powerful, wise woman with the ability to help others discover moments of magical insight within themselves. I am a truth-seeker and truth-teller, obsessed with creative potential. I am a seeker and an explorer of knowledge and of infinite possibilities. I am a practical, realistic idealist, seeking to tap into this realm of infinite possibility and translate it into tangible, useful, and applicable forms. I am a servant here to help others see their own potential and contribute it in concrete ways to maximize their impact in the world. I am a creator, a catalyst, a teacher, and a guide.

What I Believe

I believe there is unlimited potential in each of us. I believe we are more the same than different. I believe in substance over style. I believe in lifting people up instead of tearing them down. I believe in respect and reverence. I believe in universal truths that transcend nations and tribes: Love, Beauty, Kindness, Empathy, Compassion, Honesty, Equality, and Respect. I believe that our bodies are sacred and that our health is to be treated with the highest attention and care. I believe that what is in a person's heart is more important than what is in his wallet. I believe that outer appearances are deceiving. I believe that human beauty resides and is seen inside the soul. I believe that learning is freedom. I believe that the more wisdom we have, the more humble and reverent we become. I believe that nothing in the outer world is personal—it is merely a projection. I believe in love and deep connection. I believe everything is connected. I believe that we are all made of stardust. I believe in continuously learning, growing, and moving forward. I believe our notions of success and failure are both stories to explain learning. I believe we all are here to learn. I believe we have a lot more to learn.

What I Am Committed To

I am committed to fully contributing to the world in service of our highest human potential by teaching and guiding myself and others. I am committed to the creative process and sharing with others the wisdom and insights that process brings forward. I am committed to my inner wise woman and to listening to her guidance. I am committed to deep, meaningful connection and the care and feeding of my most cherished relationships. I am committed to my physical and mental health and well-being so that I can cultivate and maintain clear energy and vitality while in this physical body. I am committed to progress. I am committed to trying every moment to have my actions reflect what I say is most important. I am committed to rejecting self-doubt, defensiveness, reactivity, personalization, and insecurity when they come up in my human mind and replacing them with compassion and nurturing thoughts. I am committed to living with intention and impact and striving to live up to the infinite potential I have access to.

166

Tips for Creating Your Personal Manifesto

- Don't overthink what you write down here, as what comes to your mind first from looking at all the previous questions you answered and exercises you did should be closest to the truth.
- Don't try to capture every single thing either— just make it a document that resonates deeply with your whole self.
- Don't worry about what others will think when they read it or if it is profound or magnanimous enough. What you write is just right.

Type this on a piece of paper. Print it out. Or write it out in your own handwriting if you prefer. You can use regular white paper, paper in your favorite color, or create a fancy design on the page with a design application. Or you can draw on the page. Whatever makes it personalized and your own document. Some people in my workshop have framed it and put it in their home and work offices. Others have laminated several copies and keep it in various places. Still, others have pasted it in the notebook they carry with them and look at it daily. The key is to use this document as your compass and guide. It is a living document, not an exercise to complete and then put away in a drawer and forget about. This is your manifesto; your declaration of who you are as a whole person, what you believe in your heart of hearts, and who and what you are committed to becoming and embodying in the world. This is the beginning of integrating your wise self and your ego identity. The reclaiming of your soul. How does this homecoming feel?

Making the Change

You have spent the past three weeks doing some heavy-duty self-reflection and digging deep. You've taken an inner inventory and moved your ego mask identity aside to listen to what your wise woman has to say. You've listened deeply and intentionally and integrated her voice and made a bold declaration of who you are, what you believe, and what you are committed to. You may be feeling as if you have just been engrossed in an inner cleansing that has left you rejuvenated, revitalized, and renewed. You may feel greater clarity, more empowered and transformed.

How do you take this renewed clarity and live according to this manifesto you have birthed? How do you move forward now and actually embody the principles in this document? How do you make decisions and choices with more intention and alignment? In other words—how do you walk the talk of less ego and more soul in your day-to-day routines and life at home and at work?

How Do You *Actually* Change?

This book is not intended to make you completely uproot your life, quit your job, sell all your belongings, and go live alone on a mountain or buy and cultivate a llama farm. I am not suggesting that you neglect paying attention to your appearance, dismiss your contemporary life, and completely dismantle all the pieces of the ego identity you have built over the years. We live in a conventional world and want and need to be included and integrated into society. We must live and thrive in the outer world. We cannot merely live in our inner world. We want and are meant to make a meaningful contribution to others in service of the world we live in. To do that, we must be able to navigate the way things are in order to influence impactful change to what can be. We must straddle between both worlds and integrate the two into our whole self.

I'll share with you how I operationalize my manifesto in real life—and keep my inner wise woman in the front seat with me at all times. The reality is, I am looking for balance between my ego and my wise woman. I don't think I will ever or even want to annihilate my ego identity. What I strive to do is live with less ego and more soul. *Less ego, more soul.*

To have my wise woman take the seat beside me and navigate the path my ego is driving along. It's a partnership—with legitimate veto powers and navigation control given freely to the wise woman riding with me. My ego identity still gets feisty and testy and tries to push the wise woman aside. She is funny like that—childish in her tantrums and fits. She still pushes to prove and compare and please—and my wise woman reigns her in when she does it too much. The main difference is that my ego identity now listens to the wise woman—and quickly gets back on track rather than taking over and pushing her out.

Here's what this looks like in practice:

Appearance

I realize that how we appear to others and the image we project is important in the outer world we live in. Impression and perception are real, and there is much research to support the significance and impact of presentation on the human brain. As a result of our biological wiring, the way we present things and how we appear on the outside does play a part in our overall ability to have maximum impact. Remember, we are dealing in concrete reality, not merely aspirational ideals.

I am intentional about the impression I make and have created an outer appearance that represents me as credible to the conventional audiences I seek to influence. I add individuality and my own creative flair and appreciation of aesthetically pleasing color and style to my outer shell to express my individuality and artistic sense. I understand the subtle, unconscious, hidden messages my appearance can send, so I try to be consistent and intentional in what message I want to transmit through my appearance. So yes, I still pay attention to my appearance and the impact I want to have from the outer image I convey. Here is the big difference. I am clear that I am not, nor do I want to be Aphrodite. I am not consumed or defined by my appearance. My appearance is the shell, and I make no mistake that the shell is not where my value lies. Just like I knew in the first grade, the goddess energy I want to embody is the energy of Athena, the goddess of wisdom. I can integrate Aphrodite into the mix as needed and adjust the shell according to circumstance, but Athena rules. When there is a trade-off or a choice, she is quick to take charge and overrule Aphrodite's singular focus with how she appears.

Behavior

When it comes to my actions in all other areas of my life, I use the manifesto as my compass. Anytime I am about to do something, want to do something, or find myself at a decision or turning point, I look at that document. What would I do if I was true to this? It never fails to guide me in the right direction. If I am struggling with self-doubt or discouragement, I read my manifesto and somehow it refocuses me. If I am feeling out of alignment, fearful, emotionally drained, overwhelmed, or just plain tired, I read my manifesto. I remind myself of who I am becoming and ask myself what I need to do to honor what I wrote on this paper. It may take a day or two, but it always steers me back to center. When I act from a merely emotional place, overreact, take something too personally, or react from fear or protective impulses, reading the manifesto reminds me to step back away from my ego identity and draw on my wise self. It helps me regain composure, stand back from the daily dramas I find myself in, and stay true to the much bigger dimension we are all connected to.

It helps me pause and choose my response to whatever is happening around me, rather than merely react to it. And it also serves as a priority check. Am I spending my time on what I say I believe in and what I am committed to? When I'm not, what changes do I need to make to stay true to this bigger commitment I say I have? Am I acting in alignment with what I say is most important—or merely going through the motions. The manifesto is the tool I use to help me stay true to what I am striving for.

As a result, I have made choices that I may not have made if my wise woman was not integrated as an advisor. I chose to back away from a corporate climb and not focus on title achievement in the context of a corporate or someone else's organizational hierarchy. I recognized that the impact I wanted to have on the world was much bigger than any title could convey, and that I needed to have creative autonomy and freedom to apply that. I needed to spend my time on the things that would be most in alignment with the bigger contribution I was called to make. This informed my choice to step away from the conventional hierarchy I was moving in and create a career that would allow me to maximize that contribution.

I made my health a priority. I let my commitment to my physical health override my addiction to anything chocolate. I trained myself to be much more intentional about my food choices and my commitment to physical fitness. Was I going to walk the talk or not? If I was choosing to be in alignment with what I say is important, then I would have to make sacrifices. I couldn't have it both ways, at least not all the time.

In my interactions with others, if I truly believed what I wrote on that paper, then I would need to act accordingly. I would need to put aside personalizing interactions and step back and look at the bigger story playing out in each interaction. I would need to demonstrate that I valued the other person at a soul level—and be empathetic about their unique experience. I would have to focus on how we are alike rather than look for how we are different and try and find common ground. I would have to suspend judgment and not look for how the interaction fit with me and my experience. I would have to realize that the experience others are having in the outer world are different and create different reactions. That experience was not about me at all. I would focus on how I could contribute in the here and now, right where we are. Sometimes that is just acknowledging another's experience. Sometimes it is just being still. I didn't always need to fix things or do anything. My biggest contribution especially in the work I do is sometimes just creating a safe space for people to let go of their defenses by being vulnerable and transparent myself.

It helps me strive to live with less ego. More soul. Am I there? Absolutely not. I am a work in progress, as we all are. But I am moving forward consciously and intentionally, and each moment is another choice point.

Operationalizing Your Own Personal Manifesto

When I describe this operationalization, again, remember that I am practical. I am not suggesting that as a result of this book that you should quit your job and throw all practical caution to the wind. I am suggesting that you re-evaluate whether or not the path you are following is maximizing the contribution you are called to make. Is it aligned with who you say you are, what you believe in, and what is most important to you? It may be.

The key to moving away from your ego mask is to reevaluate everything you learned that helped you become who you are. Conventional norms and cultural stories you were socialized with are just those—stories. While they have served you well and there are values that you may want to preserve, you can no longer have those stories let you mosey through your life believing you are safe and comfortable by abiding by these beliefs. Your deeper, wiser self—your soul—knows better. Because this part of you is not separate at all. It is not governed by the stories you have learned to protect yourself. It recognizes something much deeper about all of humanity—that everything and everyone is more the same than different and universally connected.

Less Ego, More Soul

With this deeper work in this book, your ultimate goal is to move from letting your choices and actions be unconscious—ruled by the conventional and cultural norms you have been taught or socialized with—to conscious—being shaped by your inner wise self—your soul.

There is a big difference in this seemingly small distinction:

Unconscious conformity choices
I act according to conventional norms in order to:

- Be included
- Be seen as good
- Fit in
- Feel validated
- Feel in control
- Feel safe
- Please others
- Protect myself
- Win
- Achieve

Conscious conformity choices
- Understand
- Influence
- Respect
- Listen
- Do no harm
- Include
- Connect
- Contribute
- Serve

Everything we do that is of value in the world takes hard work, focus and dedication. There will be parts of whatever you do that you do not like or that are in service of your wiser self. Perhaps you are in a job that you don't like in service of your bigger contribution to your family or to what you hold most dear. Perhaps you are at a career crossroads and your current job is serving as your means to gain experience for what you want to offer in the future. Or perhaps your current job is funding your creating of art or music or of your volunteering efforts on the weekend. Being true to your wiser self doesn't mean you throw out the practical considerations of making a living. *It means that you are conscious of your why. WHY are you doing the things you do?* What bigger part of yourself are you honoring as you do what you do? What higher commitments are you operating in service of, beyond your own ego self? Being a mother, for example, maybe the contribution you are called to make in this world. Are you being conscious as you do that? Are you being true to who you say you are and what you are committed to as you do that? Who are you BEING as you DO the things you do on a daily basis?

Operating with less ego and more soul means that you are not just going through the motions and doing things because you were taught to and because you think you have to. Operating with less ego means you realize that you are much bigger than your daily dramas and that the world doesn't operate or revolve around you. It means that you are in alignment with a higher order in the world and make your moment-to-moment choices according to that bigger self.

Commitment is the glue that binds your intentions, which you will materialize with action, accountability, and impact. Go forth with who you are becoming. Live and lead with less ego and more soul.

"Live and lead with less ego and more soul."

Less Ego, More Soul

References

Co-Active Training Institute. https://coactive.com.

National Institute of Mental Health. "5 Things You Should Know About Stress."

https://www.nimh.nih.gov/health/publications/stress/index.shtml.

Psychologist World. "Carl Jung: Archetypes and Analytical Psychology."

https://www.psychologistworld.com/cognitive/carl-jung-analytical-psychology.

Less Ego, More Soul

About the Author

Janet Ioli has been helping people and organizations make changes and maximize their impact for over 25 years. As a former leader inside four Fortune 200 companies, she understands first-hand the complexities and realities leaders face leading their organizations.

Grounded in real experience working with thousands of leaders in different industries and countries and having provided over 10,000 hours of coaching, Janet has earned a reputation as an extraordinarily talented, highly results-oriented and sought-after leadership coach, change strategist, speaker, and organizational advisor. *Forbes* has recognized Janet as one of the country's leading business coaches with membership in the Forbes Coaches Council.

Janet's wealth of practical experience is backed by continuous and robust educational substance and focus, in addition to thousands of hours of self-study in psychology, leadership, change, neuroscience, and human development. She has master's degrees in both Public Administration and Business, an undergraduate degree in Business, and has extensively studied Human Development and Adult Learning at the Doctoral academic level. Janet also holds a certification from the National Board of Medical Examiners as a health and wellness professional. Janet is certified as a Professional Certified Coach by the International Coach Federation and has an Advanced Executive Coaching Certificate from the Smith School of Business and a Certificate in Positive Psychology and Well-being Coaching.

Janet partners with major universities as an industry expert in women's leadership— she is on the faculty of American University's Key Executive Leadership Program for government leaders and is a designer and speaker for the University of California at Irvine's Women in Leadership Certificate Program. As a recognized thought leader on leadership, self-development, and change, Janet is a contributor to Forbes and Thrive Global. She is the author of *The Cure, Power Presence for Women*, and *Less Ego, More Soul.*

Acknowledgements

This message I bring forward in this book has been calling me ever since I can remember. I have thought and talked about the concepts in this book as early as a senior in high school in a speech in a forensics championship competition. The speech, titled "Image, Society, and Man's Search for His Soul", won first place in the competition. I knew then as I absolutely know now, that the key to a more powerful presence in the world is to live and lead with *Less Ego, More Soul.*

Nothing we ever do in this world is done alone. It is from the contributions of the people we meet in our lives that we become who we are and answer the call to serve.

My life has been blessed with extraordinary people who have supported me and helped me birth this book— whether they realize it or not. I want to take the time to thank and acknowledge each of them:

Frank—you show me every day what a real partner and soulmate is in spirit and in the world. Your love, encouragement, support, and listening as I pontificated about the importance of this topic over the years have helped me the gain the confidence to express the message more widely. Your patience in reading draft after draft of the manuscript and your delicate yet honest and practical feedback have been a gift to me more valuable than any other.

Nicole—your presence in my life reminds me every day to love unconditionally. That love is patient. It keeps no records of wrongs. It always protects. Always trusts. Always hopes. Always perseveres. Love never fails.

Kathy—your encouragement and support is etched in my heart. I think of you often with love when I write as I follow your own journey to integrate the voice of your inner wise self into your life.

Emily—your friendship shows me that values and authentic connection bind us beyond the masks.

Ariel—your bright eyes, hopes, and dreams remind me to stay true to that childhood wonder and magic you display every day.

Gabriella – you remind me that life is way too precious to be squandered—and to have courage to write about what matters.

Karen—your encouragement to write from the heart and tell my own stories helped me express my own truth on the pages.

Ricky—your support and pep talks helped me stay true to my voice and your author photo made me look spectacular.

Candi—your expert editing made my words sing and flow more succinctly and cohesively, and your practical advice helped me keep the reader in the forefront.

Kathleen—your expert organizational skills helped me put this book into reality and create a tangible final product.

And to all the leaders, groups, students, and clients I have worked with over the years and continue to work with now—thank you for the profound lessons. You have taught me more than I could ever teach you.

Less Ego, More Soul

Made in the USA
San Bernardino, CA
12 August 2020